PUBLIC GOODS, PRIVATE GOODS

PRINCETON MONOGRAPHS

IN PHILOSOPHY

Harry Frankfurt, Editor

———————————— • ꟼMꟼ • ————————————

The Princeton Monographs in Philosophy series

offers short historical and systematic studies

on a wide variety of philosophical topics.

Justice Is Conflict by STUART HAMPSHIRE

Self-Deception Unmasked by ALFRED R. MELE

Liberty Worth the Name by GIDEON YAFFE

Public Goods, Private Goods by RAYMOND GEUSS

RAYMOND GEUSS

PUBLIC GOODS

PRIVATE GOODS

PRINCETON UNIVERSITY PRESS

Copyright © 2001 by Princeton University Press
Published by Princeton University Press, 41 William Street,
Princeton, New Jersey 08540
In the United Kingdom: Princeton University Press,
3 Market Place, Woodstock, Oxfordshire OX20 1SY

Library of Congress Cataloging-in-Publication Data

Geuss, Raymond.
Public goods, private goods / Raymond Geuss.
p.   cm.—(Princeton monographs in philosophy)
Includes bibliographical references and index.
ISBN 0-691-08903-5 (alk. paper)—
1. Liberalism. 2. Political ethics. 3. Moral conditions.
I. Title. II. Series.
JC574 .G48   2001
320.50—dc21   2001021991

This book has been composed in Janson

Printed on acid-free paper. ∞

www.pup.princeton.edu

Printed in the United States of America

1   3   5   7   9   10   8   6   4   2

CONTENTS

PREFACE

In 1984 MY THEN colleague at Princeton, Robert Maxwell, invited me to give a paper at a conference on "The Public Realm" which he was organizing at the School of Architecture (of which he was dean). This was the first time I tried to think in a sustained way about the concepts of the public and the private and their relation to each other, and I am very grateful to Robert Maxwell for providing me with that opportunity. Unfortunately my only copy of the paper I wrote was stolen from my hotel room in Belgrade in 1986, so I was especially pleased to be invited to give a talk in September 1999 at a conference here at Cambridge on "Asian and Western Conceptions of Public and Private," because it allowed me to return to this topic and have a second try at it. I gave a talk entitled "Shamelessness, Spirituality, and the Common Good," and this book is an expansion of that talk. I wish to thank the organizers of the conference, the Institute for the Integrated Study of Future Generations (Kyoto), the institute's president Tae-Chang Kim, John Dunn, and Ross Harrison for the kind invitation to speak. I have greatly benefited from discussions about the ancient world with Peter Garnsey, who also saved me from making several egregious historical mistakes. I am also much indebted to Rüdiger Bittner, Fred Neuhouser, Robert Pippin, and Bernard Williams for written comments on my draft, and to a number of colleagues and friends at Cambridge, particularly Zeev Emmerich, Hilary Gaskin, Istvan Hont, David Sedley, and Quentin Skinner, for discussion of the topics treated in this essay.

PUBLIC GOODS, PRIVATE GOODS

CHAPTER I

INTRODUCTION

IN 1814 ONE OF THE founding figures of European liberalism, Benjamin Constant, published what was to become his most influential book on politics, *De l'esprit de conquête et de l'usurpation.*[1] In it he distinguished sharply between the "private existence" of members of a modern society and their "public existence." "Private existence" referred to the family and the intimate circle of personal friends, the spheres of individual work and the consumption of goods, and the realm of individual beliefs and preferences; "public existence"[2] designated action in the world of politics. For a variety of historical, economic, and social reasons, Constant thought, the "private" sphere had come in the modern world to be the source of especially vivid pleasures, and the locus for the instantiation of especially deep and important human values. In the small self-governing city-states of antiquity the sphere of private production was tedious and laborious—an endless backbreaking round of agricul-

tural activity—and that of consumption underde-
veloped. On the other hand, the political power of
ancient democratic assemblies was virtually unlimited; in principle, such an assembly could regulate
anything. All private actions, including even such
things as how the citizens chose their occupation
or their marriage partner, how they educated their
children, or what type of crockery they had on
their tables, could in principle be, and often in
fact were, subject to severe public scrutiny and
control.[3] This power was also exercised by the citizens in assembly directly, and gave rise to a keen
experience of pleasure (and pride) which surpassed
any pleasure that could be found in private life.
Under these circumstances it made some sense for
individuals to be willing to "constitute themselves
virtually the slaves of the nation"[4] if that was the
price to be paid for having a "public existence,"
that is, being fully active citizens. Being a citizen
in an ancient democracy meant, after all, directly
wielding a real executive power, and was a full-time
occupation.[5] No modern population, Constant
claims, is willing seriously and persistently to sub-
ordinate its private existence to the demands of
politics in the way ancient democracy required; for
such populations, private goods have, and ought to
have, priority over the goods of the public realm.
This is why the "fictive"[6] form of the exercise of

popular sovereignty, representative government with limited and conditional powers of intervention in citizens' private domains, is the appropriate one for modern conditions. Such a form of government is "fictive" compared with the direct and unmediated exercise of power in ancient politics, and it is desirable because it allows moderns to retain enough indirect supervision over the political sphere to prevent gross harm, while being sufficiently undemanding of time and energy to allow citizens to direct their main attention to what is really of value to them, the good private life. Understanding this split between private and public existence and the relative standing of the values associated with each of the two spheres was, Constant believed, a precondition for understanding politics in the modern world.

Two decades before the publication of Constant's book, one of the other theoretical founders of liberalism, the German theorist von Humboldt, had written his radically antipaternalist political tract *Ideen zu einem Versuch, die Gränzen der Wirksamkeit des Staats zu bestimmen.*[7] Because the highest human good, he claimed, is the self-activity and self-development of human individuals, and the state has no value in itself but is merely a necessary means to individual self-activity, *any* positive provision for individual welfare, whether spiritual, moral, or material, on the part of the state is inappropriate and in fact actively harmful because it preempts individual action. The state therefore ought to limit its sphere of activity to maintaining security, and it should otherwise allow its members to get on with their own private lives in whatever way they choose.

Nowadays not everyone would accept the details of Constant's account of the necessities of modern politics or his normative assessments of its possibilities. Many moderns have also been tempted to try to replace Humboldt's naturalistic doctrine of the goal of human life with more deontological, especially Kantian, views, thinking these a firmer basis for antipaternalism; few would go as far in limiting the powers of the state as Humboldt suggested. Nevertheless much contemporary thinking about politics, especially self-consciously "liberal" forms of thinking, does seem to be following in the track of the tradition deriving from these two figures. The temptation to try to combine "private existence" (as the concept is understood in Constant's historical sociology) with "private life" (in the quasi-moral sense in which Humboldt uses this term) into the idea of a politically and socially distinct and protected sphere of life within which each individual is and ought to be fully sovereign,[8] and to contrast this sphere with a public world of law, economics, and politics, is a strong one.

The idea that there is a clear distinction between "public" and "private," and that this distinction is of great and continuing philosophical and political significance,[9] is not the preserve of a small number of philosophers but is well entrenched even in everyday political discussions. Around this general distinction a number of thoughts cluster. Thus some have thought that the evaluative conceptions that are appropriate for use in the public realm are different from those appropriate in the private realm. What is judged to be "good," "right," "valuable" (and, alternatively, "bad," "wrong," a "nuisance") in the public sphere is to be evaluated by very different standards from what is "good" in the private sphere. The standards and procedures for justifying a particular course of action or choice, and the audience in whose eyes the justification must be convincing, are often thought to differ depending on whether what is at issue is a "private" act (e.g., individual purchase of food for one's own consumption) or a public one (procurement of new trains for the municipal underground or new submarines for the navy). Finally there is often thought to be a series of characteristic differences between the kinds of methods and means that can legitimately be employed: in certain kinds of action in the public realm, duly constituted political authorities may use direct physical coercion (restraint, incarceration, execution, etc.) or the threat of such coercion to implement compliance with a directive in ways that would be unacceptable if used by individuals in private contexts.

I wish to argue that there is no single clear distinction between public and private but rather a series of overlapping contrasts, and thus that the distinction between the public and the private should not be taken to have the significance often attributed to it. One result of this, I think, should be a change in the way we think about the good in various public and private contexts. Although my final interest is the good, the first immediate object of my attention will be conceptions of the public and the private.

In the contemporary world one might be pardoned for assuming that the distinction between "private" and "public" is relatively straightforward. It concerns the modes of access, control, and ownership of property or information, with special reference to the issue of whether this access, control, and ownership is restricted or limited in any way. Public property is property thought to be owned in common by the unrestricted set of all the people in some given society—or by the state as representative of all the people; private property is property owned by some restricted set of individuals or even by a single individual, not owned by all in common. Public information is information to which everyone has (or ought to have) access; private acts are those to which not everyone has or ought to have cognitive access. The shift in this formulation between a descriptive version ("information to which everyone has access") and a normative version ("information to which everyone ought to have access") adds a complication but is not in any sense deeply confusing or troubling. After all, many political concepts (e.g., democracy) exhibit this vacillation. To be sure, we know that some societies have not made the same kind of binary distinction to which we are accustomed. Thus the Romans at certain periods distinguished between public, private, and sacred law (*ius*) and public, private, and sacred property, but we are not terribly concerned with the gods' property, and in any case this, too, seems a mere conservative extension of our normal usage which is made possible by the recognition of a different ontological type of agent (a god). Even in the modern world "private" is not the only opposite of "public." Thus if one is thinking of information one can also contrast "public" with "secret," which carries the connotation that the piece of knowledge in question ought to be known and is being withheld by the conscious act of some agent.[10] "Private," however, has the connotation of something that ought not to be common knowledge. One can also contrast "public" with "arcane." The "arcane," in contemporary usage, offers limited cognitive access because of its nature, not because anyone is keeping it secret or because access to it ought to be restricted.[11] A related distinction is that between "esoteric"—meant only for members of a select group—and "exoteric"—directed at those outside the group. The distinction between the public and the private, as usually understood, is not identical with that between social or collective and the individual: a meeting of friends is a social or collective phenomenon, but it can be a "private" occasion, and an individual can be a "public" figure. Similarly it is not identical with that between the altruistic and the egotistic: I can have altruistic or egotistical feelings in my relations with private friends or in the exercise of a public office. These last claims are familiar and do not, I assume, require elaboration here.

My title, *Public Goods, Private Goods*, is intentionally ambiguous. "Goods" can mean several things. First, it can designate concrete objects that have some use-value: a pen I own is a private good; a bridge built with governmental funds and usable

by all is a public good. Second, it can be taken ab-
stractly as meaning "that which is, or is considered
to be, good." So the fact that the streets are secure
and safe may be a public good; that I have spent
an enjoyable evening in conversation with a friend
might be an instance of a private good. In neither
of these cases is the "good" in question an object.
Third, "goods" can mean "conceptions of the
good," and the adjectives "public" and "private"
can then be construed either as equivalent to what
grammarians used to call "subjective" or to "objective" genitives, that is, as meaning "one conception
(among a possible variety of conceptions) of the
good held *by* the public" or "one conception
(among a possible variety of conceptions) of that
which is good *for* the public."

Argumentation is an important part of politics,
moral reflection, and social life in general, and the
philosophical study of politics has understandably
focused on technical analysis of the stringency and
plausibility of the arguments presented by theorists. Politics, however, also contains other elements that one could call rhetorical, motivational,
or ideological; because of their practical importance, these elements do not deserve to be completely ignored. Thus there are perfectly good arguments that do not convince; arguments that,
although they carry a kind of conviction, fail to

motivate; finally there are considerations, arguments, and ways of seeing the world that *seem* irre-
sistibly plausible (and perhaps also motivationally
compelling) at a certain time to members of certain groups, although outsiders can see in them
only tissues of delusion or theoretically ad hoc
constructions.

The public/private distinction is such an ideological concretion. Disparate components—conceptual fragments, theories, folk reactions, crude
distinctions that are useful in highly specific practical contexts, tacit value assumptions—from different sources and belonging to different spheres
have come together historically in an unclear way
and have accumulated around themselves a kind of
capital of self-evidence, plausibility, and motivational force. The unreflective use of distinctions
such as this one restricts our possibilities of per-
ceiving and understanding our world. It also can
have the effect of casting a vague glow of approba-
tion on highly undeserving features of our world
or possible courses of action (or, alternatively, of
shining the blinding light of unwarranted suspi-
cion on possibilities we would do well to consider
sympathetically). Unraveling the connections between different senses of "private" and "public"
can help break the hold the public/private distinction has on our minds and allow us to see that po-

litical and moral options are available to us that might have been more difficult to see, or to evaluate positively, before.

The various senses in which the terms *public* and *private* are and have been used are numerous, much more numerous and varied than I could coherently discuss in a brief essay. Rather than proceeding either by trying to sketch fully the history of the various ways the terms *public* and *private* have been used or trying to draw further abstract distinctions between these senses, I would like instead to begin by discussing three more or less concrete instances of human behavior. Each instance is an action performed by a known historical figure who lived in the Mediterranean basin during the period we call "Antiquity," and each illustrates an aspect of our conception of the public and the private. Since my point is precisely the *lack* of a single unitary intuition informing these varying conceptions, I need not (and do not) claim either historical or conceptual completeness for my account.

CHAPTER II

SHAMELESSNESS
AND THE
PUBLIC WORLD

D IOGENES OF SINOPE, who lived in the fourth
century B.C., was in the habit of masturbating
in the middle of the Athenian marketplace.[1] He
was not pathologically unaware of his surroundings, psychotic, or simple-minded. Nor was he living in a society that stood at the very beginning of
what Elias[2] calls "the process of civilization"; that
is, he was not living in a society fairly low on what
we take to be the scale of our cultural evolution,
one in which such forms of behavior were not yet
subject to systematic disapproval and socially regulated. Rather, we know that the Athenians objected
to his mode of life in general and to this form of
behavior in particular. They clearly considered
him a kind of public nuisance and made their disapproval known to him. We know this because the

doxographic tradition specifically records Diogenes' response to a criticism of his masturbating in
public. He is said to have replied that he wished
only that it were as easy to satisfy hunger by just
rubbing one's belly.[3]

Why, exactly, was this action offensive? I suggest
three distinct reasons. First, it has been argued
convincingly that many societies, including, notably, most contemporary Western European societies, are governed by a tacit principle about how
one is to comport oneself in public places that has
been called the principle of "civil inattention" or
"disattendability."[4] A public place is a place where
I can expect to be observed by "anyone who happens to be there," that is, by people I do not know
personally and who have not necessarily given
their explicit consent to entering into close interaction with me. The marketplace in an ancient city
is, par excellence, such a public environment: different people, who will not necessarily be known
to one another, and who, at one level, have different, unpredictable, and perhaps incompatible purposes, preferences, and tastes, come into physical
proximity with one another, each pursuing his or
her own distinct business. The principle of disattendability states that in such contexts and places I
am to be unobtrusive or, at any rate, to avoid being
systematically obtrusive. In other words, I am to

allow the other whom I may encounter to disattend to me, to get on with whatever business he or
she has without needing to take account of me. I
am not to force myself on anyone's attention. Masturbating is an action we would normally classify
as voluntary, but the principle of disattendability
extends to all features of me that might call attention to themselves, even those not at all subject to
my control, such as lacking a nose; that is, it applies
before or *below* the level at which we distinguish
the voluntary from the involuntary. Thus a pair of
Siamese twins joined at the head who appear in
public by going shopping violate the rule of disattendability even though they are in no sense
responsible for the condition that makes them
violate the rule.[5] They may be thought to violate
the rules of behavior in public simply by being the
way they are; their very existence can, as it were,
be construed as an automatic affront. Violations
of the principle of disattendability seem to fall
into two groups: (a) stigmas in the strict sense, that
is, "natural" (as we would call them) features that
cannot be changed by those who have them
(whether congenital, as with Siamese twins, or acquired, as with the loss of one's nose in an acci-
dent) or social (being born in the wrong place, having the wrong kind of surname, etc.); and (b)
failures of competence. The second group in turn

includes: (1) violations resulting from ignorance about what competence it is appropriate to exercise (not knowing that one genuflects in the direction of the altar in a particular church); (2) violations resulting from failure to acquire a competence (never having learned the complex "leg discipline" that governs behavior in public); (3) violations resulting from fatigue, momentary lapse of attention, etc.; (4) voluntary failure to exercise a competence that one has; and (5) willful violation with the intention of insulting those present.[6] Diogenes violates this principle of disattendability, certainly voluntarily and probably willfully, and so acts in an offensive way.

The second reason why Diogenes' action is offensive is that many societies hold not just to the principle of disattendability in public places but *also* to a principle of avoiding near occasions of envy; that is, it is thought to be inappropriate to exhibit the satisfaction of certain basic, imperative human needs in the presence of others if that satisfaction is problematic, precarious, or otherwise not to be taken for granted. Thus in many preindustrial societies one *never* eats in the presence of someone else who is not also eating, and I suggest that the reason for this, at least in part, is because food is a relatively scarce and uncertain good in some societies. Diogenes is also reported to have been reproached for eating in the market-place.[7] Historically as food becomes more plenti-ful, this taboo also often relaxes.[8] Sexual gratifi-cation can be seen to have a similar structure, given the way social and other factors restrict op-portunities in many societies. Thus there is a taboo on showing that one is being or has recently been sexually satisfied in a public place where others are present who may not be, or may not have re-cently been, thus gratified.[9] Diogenes violates this taboo, too.

To see the third reason for the offensiveness of Diogenes' action, it is useful to recall another story told about him. One day, it is reported, he was dis-coursing in the marketplace, trying to instruct the Athenians on how one ought to live one's life; when no one paid him any attention, he began to whistle. People gathered around, and he then be-rated them for paying attention to the senseless noise of someone whistling when they paid no at-tention to philosophical instruction.[10] Whistling, because it is hard to ignore, violates the principle of disattendability, but under normal circum-stances it generates no envy. Masturbating is pre-sumably also hard to ignore, and sexual gratifica-tion is a possible object of envy, but Diogenes' action offends in yet another way, and this further dimension is the third reason why Diogenes' be-

havior is offensive: the action that calls attention
to itself is not simply an action that is in itself relatively innocuous, like speaking in an excessively
loud voice, whistling, or eating, but it is an action
that is inherently connected with the production of a substance thought by many to be dirty,
disgusting, or polluting.[11] Humans, that is, make
a distinction between two broad categories of
things: the pure, clean, or fair and the foul, polluted, or dirty.[12] In response to the foul, polluted,
or dirty, we have one of a series of possible negative reactions ranging from a mild disinclination
through distaste and active avoidance to the extreme disgust that expresses itself in violent retching. If I involuntarily vomit up something presented to me as food, my body is unambiguously
refusing it. Vomiting up something is somatically
asserting in a very vivid way that that thing is "different" from me; it is drawing a barrier between
myself and the "food." In many societies I can spit
as a similar expression of a slightly more intellectu-
alized disgust, thereby distancing myself morally
from a kind of behavior of which I disapprove.[13]
The objects of these negative reactions that are of
interest to me in this context are certain human
bodily activities, such as eating, drinking, excret-
ting, or secreting; certain objects associated with
these activities; and then, by extension, certain

sights, feels, smells, textures, and tastes that call to mind these bodily activities or their products and concomitants.[14] Many of the basic bodily activities that call forth this reaction are ones that are central to our well-being but that are also associated with forms of human vulnerability.[15] They often concern things on the boundary between the inside and the outside of the human body. For all these reasons they are a natural and understandable locus of feelings of anxiety.[16] Although reactions of avoidance and disgust seem to be rooted in basic facts of human biology and exist in all human societies, the particular form they take is culturally shaped and is acquired only through a long process of training. Children do not need to be taught to withdraw their hands when they put them in a fire, but they notoriously *do* need to be taught to have the proper reactions of disgust to their own excrement.[17]

The way that this categorial distinction between the pure/clean, on the one hand, and the polluting/filthy, on the other, is drawn may differ from person to person and from society to society, and the intensity and exact nature of the reaction that the polluting elicits will also vary. What causes merely a mild avoidance reaction in one person may cause active retching in a more fastidious member of a society of a certain kind.[18] Thus it is often said that the taboos on urinating in public are less strict (for men at any rate) in Japan than in the West, but that Japanese find any touching or scratching of the nose highly disgusting. Nevertheless the variation does not seem to be fully and simply random (in the way that more strictly cultural variation is). Although taboos on urinating in public may be looser in Japan, they do exist; one would not urinate just anywhere. There does seem to be a set of humanly shared, more central phenomena that will be the objects of disgust if anything is, and will be the objects of the strongest disgust, and there also seems to be a kind of order of disgust. Almost any-one who is capable of being disgusted by anything is disgusted by feces or cannibalism; many people in many cultures (but not all people in all cultures) are disgusted by blood; and slightly fewer are re-pelled by rank smells, and so forth.

It is curious that although disgust almost surely has its basis in some deeply rooted biological reac-tions, it is not just culturally highly malleable as far as its object is concerned; it also has a peculiar transformative power and is symbolically highly transferable. If I give my neighbor poison, I harm her; if I give her a picture of poison, I do not (gen-erally speaking) harm or even offend her. In stark contrast, while real feces directly provokes strong disgust, pictures of feces often evoke a milder version of the same reaction, and in some societies even words for feces are to be used with care. Thus one can see that Diogenes might provoke disgust even were the semen he produced not visible—the very fact that bystanders *knew* he was masturbating might provoke in them at least a mild version of the full revulsion they would feel had they actually seen the semen. The structure of disgust, then, is like the structure of certain forms of primitive magic. Disgust can render its objects so magically contagious that they infect anything even indirectly or ideationally associated with them, causing mild reactions of revulsion even to representations of disgusting objects, even to the mere knowledge that something disgusting was taking place.

Finally, a strong interpersonal component seems to play a role in these reactions in that many things that would disgust me if someone else did them do not always disgust me when I do them. Even a person of great and delicate sensibility may, in some circumstances, pick her own nose without any visible signs of distress, although she would be deeply disgusted by such behavior in someone else.

In the interpersonal realm, a rough correlation exists between certain forms of disgust and shame.[19] Diogenes should be ashamed of doing what he does in a place where others can see him. In our society, the generation of intimacy is often connected with overcoming the normal boundaries of disgust, so that intimate friends do things in one another's presence without shame (on the one hand) and disgust/ offense (on the other) that they would not do in the presence even of good acquaintances, that is, of people who are not simply anonymous others but persons whom they know, and perhaps even like, but who are not special and intimate friends. This can be connected with the notion that an intimate friend becomes, as it were, a "part" of me, and so I extend my lack of disgust from my own bodily smells, secretions, and so on, to encompass those of the intimate friend.[20] I do not think this is a precisely correct account of intimacy, at least between adults, because it overlooks a crucial distinction, namely, the distinction between things for which I never develop feelings of shame and disgust—unless I am extremely disturbed, I will never have developed a reaction of disgust to my own urinating—and the process of overcoming a barrier that is established between people. It is part of the pleasure that a devotee of "high" game or of strong cheeses experiences to overcome the ever so slight revulsion that could be caused by the smell. The existence of the barrier itself is part of the attraction and contributes to the pleasure experienced in overcoming it.[21]

Since others, however, may generally be more fastidious than I am, and even those who are no more fastidious may find things *I* do offensive, although I find them unobjectionable (when *I* do them), we classify many actions as the kinds of things that ought to be performed only where they are not noticeable to others, that is, where others cannot see, hear, touch, or smell them. That is what is meant by performing things "only in private." As a decent person, in other words, I take account of the fear others may have of being sullied or disgusted by my actions and therefore do not force them to observe certain things I do. I may have a concern for another's possible reactions even if I think them ungrounded or excessive. This is one point at which this discussion is connected with the issue of tolerance. I do not simply tolerate that others behave differently, smell bad, and so on, but I also actively accept that sociability imposes on me a requirement of self-restraint which I might myself find superfluous. Being myself of a relatively robust and insouciant constitution, *I* would probably not be much bothered if we all stank like goats, but still I wash. Note that toleration here will probably have a rather different structure from the toleration of divergent *opinions* which has been central to much liberal thinking.[22] Usually I am thought to have better or less good grounds for my opinions, but I do not always have "grounds" in any analogous sense for simple reactions of disgust.

Diogenes' conscious flouting of this principle of decency and consideration for others is connected with his pursuit of an ideal of individual self-suffi-ciency. There are, of course, in principle, at least three distinct ways of trying to attain self-suffi-ciency, first by reducing one's needs and desires so as to make them easily attainable by one's own efforts, and, second, by increasing one's powers. The third possibility is to combine both of these in some way. Diogenes adopted this third ap-proach but gave pride of place within the synthesis to the first. The mere unvarnished advice, how-ever, to try to reduce one's desires and needs is not really sufficiently determinate and informative to be a useful guide on how to live one's life. It is self-defeating to try to reduce one's desire for food below a certain minimal level, and how then do I know *which* of my desires and needs I should try to reduce and to what level? On this issue Diogenes is a rationalist. He believes that "right reason" (ὀρθὸς λόγος) will show us that some needs and desires are unavoidable, necessary, and imperative, like the basic human bodily needs that must be satisfied if human life is to be maintained. It makes no sense to try to get rid of these, although, of course, it might make good sense to consider in what way and to what extent some bodily needs, such as hunger, are to be satisfied. Diogenes calls these needs and desires that can be seen as rationally necessary "natural" (needs, desires, etc.). Such natural needs (and desires), he thought, were relatively easy to satisfy and were to be strictly distinguished from the needs and desires that arise by convention, that is, that are engendered in us by forces in human society. Hunger is a natural need and can be satisfied with a wide variety of things that come to hand; the desire to dine off porcelain is conventional. Conventional or artificial needs are overwhelmingly those that we cannot easily satisfy by ourselves. If we then can learn to restrict ourselves to natural needs, we will end up with a budget of needs that is as close as we can get to one that will allow us to be self-sufficient. Precisely because artificial or conventional needs are not imposed on us by natural necessity, one might think it should be relatively easy to rid ourselves of them, but Diogenes does not think that we can attain the ideal of self-sufficiency without effort or training (*as-kesis*).[23] We can distinguish three parts to Diogenes' *"askesis."* First, Diogenes subjected himself to the usual training in bearing with the natural rigors and inconveniences of human life, that is, in controlling natural reactions to changes in the surrounding environment. Thus as humans we suffer from extremes of temperature, but with some practice, it is claimed, we can make ourselves less bothered by such external states of temperature. So Diogenes is reported to have practiced embracing statues in the winter to accustom himself to bearing the cold. Second, we can try to overcome socially inculcated, but merely conventional, reactions to possible ways of satisfying our natural needs. Thus many societies inculcate in their members an aversion to eating human flesh, even the flesh of healthy young people who die in accidents. Overcoming socially generated prejudices like these is, Diogenes thinks, an integral part of the philosopher's task.[24] Third, and finally, there are socially generated needs strictly so called, like the need for a good reputation, that is, for the good opinion of one's fellows. One important way that one maintains the good opinion of others is precisely by observing the usual rules of decent behavior. These rules will be of the form that one "ought to be ashamed to . . . (e.g., eat human flesh, defecate in public)." In Diogenes' view, if human flesh is nourishing and easily available, I should, if I am trying to lead a good life, try to overcome my aversion to eating it, but if I am living in a society like those in which most of us have grown up, overcoming my own aversion will not be the end of the story. Even if I have no reaction of disgust or revulsion, others might have such a reaction. We often take this as a reason not to do certain things in public. Actually there might be two slightly different reasons: (a) decency demands that I not subject others to situations that will arouse their disgust—even if that disgust is based on a false view, such as that cannibalism is contrary to divine law, or, *within limits*, on a personal fastidiousness slightly more excessive than my own; and (b) prudence demands that I be concerned with what others think of me, because if they hold me in contempt because of my personal habits or public behavior, they may not come to my aid in moments of need. The first of these is a demand to have positive consideration for others, the second a demand that arises out of fear that I will fail to get assistance I might need. Diogenes rejects both these reasons. Canons of decency are artificial and thus irrational, and the truly self-reliant person has no need of others, so the argument from prudence fails.

Self-sufficiency requires, then, both the "positive" development of my powers and at the same time the "negative" reduction of my needs to those

that are "natural." Further it requires the elimina-
tion of *all* needs merely social in origin. Since the
inculcation of a sense of shame, the uncomfortable
feeling I have when I am seen, or imagine myself
to be seen, to violate a principle of social decency
is the main mechanism by which I become bound
to the artificial needs that society generates in me,
true self-sufficiency requires complete shamelessness. The model for the second, negative part
of my task as an incipient philosopher is the dog,
which ignores human social conventions and is
completely free of any form of shame. From the
dog (κύων) the followers of Diogenes acquired
their name: Cynics. Complete shamelessness—
learning to ignore others' negative reactions of
disgust at one's appearance and behavior—is the
only true road to the self-sufficiency that is the distinguishing characteristic of the good human life.
The Cynics considered Herakles[25] to be a kind of
precursor and patron saint of their mode of life,
because they saw him as the archetype of the self-
sufficiency they sought. There are, however, two
marked differences between Herakles and Diogenes. First, Herakles made no attempt to reduce his
needs and desires. He was, on the contrary, notorious for his crude and unbridled passions, especially
for his monstrous gluttony, and, given his great

strength, he could easily afford to indulge him-self.[26] Second, Herakles was dependent on no one because of his great power, but, in the standard versions at any rate, his life was devoted to "*Kul-turarbeit*" of an altruistic, even if not strictly politi-cal, kind. His characteristic "labor" is freeing a community from the scourge of a monster that ravages it, thereby conferring on the population a distinct communal benefit. The Cynics adopted the goal of self-sufficiency (αὐτάρκεια) without the altruism.

To follow the Cynic path is to be deeply unpolit-ical in two senses. First, by aspiring to complete self-sufficiency one tries to remove oneself from the state of mutual dependence on other humans, which is one of the basic preconditions of politics. Second, to assume an attitude of complete indiffer-ence to others' opinions, and especially to behave in ways one knows others will find disgusting, is consciously to produce in others the experience of a barrier and tacitly to give them to understand that one expects to be able to do without their as-sistance, an assumption they might, justifiably or not, find insulting. To act with calculated indiffer-ence to particular others in particular circum-stances is a political ploy that may succeed or fail in its effect, but to erect such barriers consciously, systematically, and universally to all others in all circumstances is to try to position oneself outside the realm of politics. Diogenes, to be sure, coined the term *cosmopolitan*—"citizen of the universe"— to describe himself,[27] but his cosmopolitan citizenship is of a purely negative kind. When the Cynic claims not to be a citizen of *this* or *that* particular city, it is not because he envisages an all-encompassing city of which he *is* a citizen; it is because he thinks there is no such thing as a form of political organization concretely embodied anywhere, or even imaginable, of which one could even in principle rationally wish to be a citizen. Cynic "cosmopolitanism" thus amounts to no more than the rejection of any concrete political engagement in or with the world around him. It is, of course, perfectly possible to adopt the Cynic aspiration to overcome shame in the sense of not *feeling* shame at doing things that were conventionally considered to be shameful, while at the same time not *acting* publicly in such a way as to thrust one's lack of subjective shame on the attention of others in a way they would find offensive. There seems, though, to have been a strong didactic element in the way that Diogenes thrust his shamelessness on others.[28] Socrates could have been construed as doing something similar in living the kind of life he did. Unsympathetic observers saw him as an idle, interfering busybody; such hyperactive meddling (πολυπραγμοσύνη)[29] was itself a violation of the canons of polite behavior that are a refinement of the principle of civil inattention. Socrates, however, although in the heat of an argument he is sometimes accused of being disgusting,[30] is not really shameless. In Plato's *Apology* Socrates asserts that he is so busy obeying the god's injunction to investigate claims to wisdom that he has no time for the affairs of the city or his own,[31] so he takes no part in the everyday politics of Athens,[32] but he is also the opposite of a cosmopolitan. He was well known for never leaving Athens, never even going outside the city walls,[33] except when on military service, and Plato has him refuse, on the grounds of his attachment and loyalty to the city, either to propose exile from Athens as a punishment in place of execution or to escape from prison, even though this was possible.[34] Plato's Socrates claims that he is a public benefactor who deserves to be given free dinners by the πόλις because of the good he has done the city,[35] and in the *Gorgias*[36] Socrates is made to describe himself as the only true politician Athens has. His mode of life is as a series of political acts par excellence, because his action is aimed not at filling the city with new harbors, new

theaters, and new stadia, or gaining Olympic victo-
ries, but at improving the souls of the Athenians.
It is hard to see how Diogenes could have made a
similar claim for his behavior. In this, too, Diogenes seems to be an exaggeration of a trait the germ
of which can be found in Socrates, in this case a
didacticism about the good life for the individual
that can lead toward an exit from the world of politics altogether. As Plato (according to Diogenes
Laertius) said, Diogenes of Sinope was "Socrates
gone mad."[37]

We can truly say that Diogenes did "in public"
what we (and the Athenians) think ought to be
done only "in private," despite the fact that the
Athenians did not have individual words for our
concepts of "public" or "private." When we say
Diogenes did something "in public," they said he
did it "in the ἀγορά." Once we have the concepts
of "public" and "private" we can retrospectively
apply them even to cases involving agents who had
no analogous concepts, provided there is sufficient
similarity in the situations in question and provided the agents have sufficiently similar reactions
and attitudes. In this particular case we have ample
evidence that the Athenians did have a reaction
similar to one familiar to us from our own time
and that they connected it with similar properties

of the situation—that Diogenes' action took place
in conditions where it could hardly fail to be no-
ticed by people who were not intimate friends of
his (that is, in the ἀγορά).

In conclusion, then, there seem to be two
slightly different notions of "public/private" here,
corresponding to the two reasons why Diogenes'
behavior is offensive. In sense (a), the "public"
space is the area "anyone" can enter and to which
the principle of disattendability applies, and "the
public" are those people whom I allow to get on
with their affairs without disturbing them; a "private space" is one where I need not worry about
violating the principle of disattendability, and a
"private friend" (to use a somewhat old-fashioned
phrase) is someone who is not just an anonymous
"anyone" but someone with whom my relations go
beyond those governed solely by the principle of
civil inattention—I may stop to chat with this
friend even if doing so calls attention to myself. In
fact, if I encounter someone I know in the marketplace and treat that person as a stranger—fail to
greet him or her—that action may in this case
count as insulting. Two principles seem to be operating concurrently here: that I acknowledge
friends and acquaintances, and that I allow strang-
ers to disattend to me. In sense (b), "the public"
are those whom I take special care not to offend by

potentially polluting actions, even if I know them personally (but not intimately); the "private sphere" encompasses my intimate friends. Thus at a dinner party among professional colleagues a parent may say to a child, who has used an especially rude or vulgar expression or launched into a detailed description of certain bodily functions: "We don't say that (or, don't discuss that) in public." In sense (a) a dinner party is not a public occasion, but in sense (b) it is.

CHAPTER III

RES PUBLICA

The second piece of human behavior I wish to discuss comes from the late Roman Republic. In late 50 B.C. the Senate voted to declare the proconsul in Gaul, C. Julius Caesar, an outlaw and authorized the consul to raise troops against him unless he gave up his military command, handed over his troops to a designated successor, and returned to Rome alone as a "private citizen" to stand trial for various political irregularities.[1] The Romans made a rather clear verbal and conceptual distinction between public and private, and our words in English for this distinction are in fact derived from the corresponding terms in Latin.[2] Thus one term the Romans used for the entity to which political activity is mainly directed is "*res publica*." If Caesar failed to give up his troops and return for trial, he would be declared an enemy of the *res publica*.[3]

The "*publica*" component in *res publica* derives from "*populus*" (or, earlier, "*poplus*"), whose original meaning is not completely clear. The *Oxford Latin Dictionary* also connects "*publicus*" (*s.v.*) with "*pubes*," which, an adjective, it defines as:

1 Physically mature, grown up, b. (as sb.) a grown-up person, adult
2 (of plants, fruits, etc.) Full of sap or juice

and, as a noun:

1 The adult population or other aggregation of able-bodied persons, manpower, company, etc.
2 The age or condition of puberty
3 The pubic region, the private parts; the pubic hair

So, originally perhaps, the "public" and the privates (and the "public" and the "pubic") were not all that far apart; the *populus* would be all the men/boys with sap in them. Similarly Hölscher, citing the original close connection between the political and the military in which the military is usually the dominant partner, suggests that *populus* means all those (boys/men) who are capable of taking their place in the ranks of fighters, that is, "the army," or rather "those who will make up the legions" (if they are called out) or "the assembled men capable of bearing arms."[4] So *publicus* would originally have meant something like "belonging to the whole people," that is, those who make up the army. We in the early twenty-first century looking back may wish to distinguish clearly between (a) the men/boys who would be capable of bearing arms; (b) the people as a whole, that is, the whole population (of Rome); and (c) the body of citizens. "*Ciues*" presumably comes to refer eventually to (c), and the suggestion I am considering here is that although *populus*, strictly speaking, originally refers to (a), in the early period the connection between (a) and (c) is so close, and the elision of (b) under (a) and (c) so unproblematic, that it is easy to understand how the reference of *populus* could be unclear and to some extent indeterminate.

Res publica, "the army's thing," is, in the early period, systematically ambiguous as between: (a) the property of the army, especially the land it conquers and is construed as holding in common (the "*ager publicus*"), and then, as *populus* shifts from meaning concretely the body of men under arms to the whole population, *res publica* comes to mean the common property of Roman citizens, including the temples, aqueducts, city walls, streets, and so on, of Rome; (b) the status quo of power relations that exist among Romans; (c) matters of common concern to all Romans; and, finally, (d) the common good of all Romans. The meaning of "*res*" here ranges from the very concrete in (a) (property, land, objects) to the abstract in (c) and (d) ("matters of concern" or "the common good"). "*Common*" in (c) and (d) is to be taken as a serious component of their meaning. So matters of common concern are not merely things that affect each and every member of the army, though perhaps they affect each individually, such as that each one will eventually die, but things that will affect the group as a group, such as defeat at the hands of the Veiians. The common good is not the increase in the number of cows each citizen possesses but an increase in the number of temples and bridges usable by all. Since obviously one of the main factors of common concern to the *populus* is its own strength and health, the continued maintenance of that vitality and strength is a clear common good, although, as societies become more complex and differentiated, there may be disagreement about what constitutes social and political "health" and how it may best be ensured. Most ancient societies were, then, clearly aware that it was in the common good that the young be trained to be good citizens (and soldiers), and, to the extent that was the case, the "well-being" of the individuals who made up the civic body was of evident common concern. This, however, was a concern only with a certain rather restricted range of aspects of "well-being": it was a concern not with the individual per

se or with the well-being of individuals for its own
sake or for their own sake, but only *as* elements of
the political society. With increasing sophistica-
tion, people can eventually come to believe that
the best way to ensure the vitality of society is by
ensuring the well-being of the constituent members in the *widest* possible sense, and that may
mean leaving it up to them to determine themselves in what their human flourishing consists.
Still, there is a significant conceptual distinction
between taking an interest in the strength and
health of the young *as potential citizens*, because
only a political association composed of flourishing members can be vital, and the usual liberal
view that the well-being of the individuals (we
could almost say "as *priuati*")[5] is politically important in and of itself[6] as, perhaps, the goal and
rationale of the state. As Constant pointed out,[7]
the ancients could take the line they did so robustly
because they thought the life of the full citizen was
clearly the best life *for* individuals; thus in doing
what was needed to cause the city to flourish, they
were also ipso facto doing what would best enable
the individual citizens to lead the best life accessible to them.[8]

In modern societies the notion of the common
or public good tends, then, to be expanded to include a large number of things that have to do with

the individual good of the members. This may be a result of the specifically liberal ontological thesis that any political good *must* be, finally, the good of some individual (or the sum of the goods of individuals), a moral view that individual interest ought to take priority over social interest, or it may be a descendant of the ancient political view that the society as a whole will flourish only if its members are healthy, vital, and energetic—have sap in them. Conceptions of the political good that were distributive in the "modern" way, that is, that focused on individuals per se, were not completely unknown in the ancient world. A famous story[9] relates that the Athenians discussed how to use the windfall discovery of a rich vein of silver in the Laurium silver mines. One proposal was that the profits be divided and distributed equally to each Athenian citizen. Themistokles' counterproposal that a fleet of ships be built—ships that are said eventually to have been used to defeat the Persians at the battle of Salamis—carried the day, but the Athenians had mechanisms for dealing with people who made proposals that were considered out of bounds, the γραφὴ παρανόμων being the most notorious,[10] and there is no report that these mechanisms were put into operation in this case against those proposing distribution of the revenue or that these persons were in any way doing something

that was considered unusual or outrageous. Still, it
seems fair to say that on a theoretical level such an
individualist conception is virtually absent from
the extant literature. The one great exception to
this generalization is Perikles' funeral speech in
Thucydides' *Peleponnesian War* (2.35–46). Even in
this speech one does not find the characteristic
modern liberal conception that the individual self-
evidently comes first as the autonomous starting
point for theorizing and valuation, and that the political community has a right to exist *only* insofar
as it contributes to the individual's security, welfare, self-development, and so on. Perikles starts
with the ancestors and the city as a whole, and
seems keen to keep two dimensions in balance as
equals—the "freedom" of the individual citizen
and the self-assertion of the city (from which follows the demand that, when necessary, the citizens
be willing to sacrifice themselves). Thucydides has
his Perikles praise Athenian tolerance of the personal quirks of fellow citizens in everyday life but
also has him cite, with apparent approval, the common Athenian view that a person who does not
take an active part in politics (an ἰδιώτης) is a "use-
less" (ἀχρεῖος i.e., [almost] "worthless") person.
The culmination of the speech (2.41.19–26) can
be read as a paean of aggressive philistinism: The

Athenians are admired and will continue to be admired and do not need any Homer to praise them. The reason for this admiration is, "We've forced our way in (τόλμη καταναγκάσαντες) everywhere, to every place on earth or sea, and wherever we've been, we've put up reminders of the bad things we can do (and also the good), permanent ones (μνημεῖα κακῶν τε κἀγαθῶν ἀίδια)."

The distinction between senses (c) and (d) of *res publica* cited above is also especially important. Even if there is no common good, there can be matters of common concern, at least in the trivial sense that there can be things that affect the *populus* in a vital way, yet for which there is no "good" on which everyone can agree. A famine is of common concern to all because it affects the group as a whole, but there may be no policy that is agreed on nor one that deserves to be agreed on that would be good for the collectivity. Although the Romans had a clear notion of the common good, they had no concept of "the state" as a separate abstract structure of powers,[11] distinct from an actual set of people who held those positions of power; so when Caesar is accused of attacking the *res publica*, that means the status quo of power also assumed to be of common concern to all Romans and to constitute a kind of common good, that is, *res publica* in senses (b), (c), and (d) described above. If Caesar's opponents had effective control over the city of Rome, a military attack on their forces would also be likely to damage the common property of the Romans, their bridges, city walls, granaries, and so on, that is, the *res publica* in sense (a).

If there are things of common concern,[12] that is, matters that concern the safety and well-being of everyone in the group rather than that of any particular individual or subgroup, then it might, under certain circumstances, make sense to designate particular individuals (or groups) to pay particular attention to these matters and take care of them. Persons who were thus designated to discharge what can now be called "public tasks" are said to hold a "public office"; the Romans called such persons "magistrates" and saw them as being vested with "public" authority, that is, with an authority over matters of common concern to the whole people. "Public" here could still be construed as ambiguous, that is, as designating (a) the realm within which authority and power are held: "public authority" is authority *over* some matter of concern to the whole people;[13] or (b) the origin or source of legitimacy of power or authority: "public" authority is authority in some sense deriving from the whole people. Conceptually these are two quite different matters. It is also striking perhaps that one of the standard phrases for designating the source of authority in Rome is SPQR: *"The Senate and the Roman Army/People."* Senatorial sources certainly suggest that they saw the Senate as a distinct locus of authority. If "Senate" does come from *"senex"* (old man), then it would also make sense that superannuated elders, no longer capable of active military service, might be consti- tuted into an advisory body with great authority.[14] However one finally resolves this issue, it is clear that the "public" standing of the magistrates com- prises authority over matters concerning the com- mon good. The term *priuatus* is used to refer to someone who is not a holder of such a magistracy and therefore had no public authority or power. Thus one can immediately construct three senses of *priuatus* parallel to the senses of *publicus* ana- lyzed above. *Res priuata* could mean (a′) property belonging to an individual, who is not a magis- trate,[15] rather than to the army/people as a whole; (c′) a matter of concern only to an individual, who is not a magistrate, and not to the people as a whole; and (d′) the good of an individual, who is not a magistrate, and not of the whole people. There seems to be no obvious analogue to sense

(b) of *publicus*, or is it perhaps revolutionary disposition (*cupiditas rerum nouarum*) that is the arche-
typal "private thing" in this sense?

This may be clear enough, then, to distinguish
the *res* of the whole Roman people—a bridge or
freedom from famine—from the *res* of a Roman
who held no magistracy at all—his individual land
and its prosperity. This distinction, however, immediately highlights a potential difficulty, namely, that
the distinction between *priuatus* and *publicus* does
not in itself provide a clear and informative discrim-
ination in the important case of a person who *is* the
holder of a magistracy. Is that person's good a public or a private good? It seems hard to see how it
could be a private good, given that it is not the good
of a *priuatus* because the person in question is *ex
hypothesi* a holder of a magistracy. The Romans were
quick to adopt the (originally Greek) idea of distinguishing between Cicero qua office holder and Cicero qua natural human being, and identifying the
latter with the *"priuatus."*[16] They had a relatively
clear conceptual grasp on the distinction between
the holder of an office and the office itself, despite
their lack of a concept of the "state" and despite
the fact that they lacked the technical and institutional apparatus (e.g., a system of regular salaries
for magistrates, a body of professionally trained
and independent auditors, technologies for quick

communication and surveillance, etc.) that would have enabled them actually to enforce this distinction in all contexts and on all occasions.[17]

When Caesar heard of the senatorial decree, he began to move his troops back toward Rome, but he hesitated at the river Rubicon on the border between Gaul and Italy. If we are to trust historical reports, he well knew that crossing into Italy would initiate a civil war, and he made no attempt to hide this fact. Even more extraordinary are the grounds he cited for his course of action. At the crucial moment he is reported to have said:

> If I don't cross this river, I'm in trouble;
> if I do, everyone in the world is in trouble.
> Let's go![18]

He further makes it clear that the "trouble" he would be in would be that his *dignitas* would be diminished, and his great merits unrecognized and unrewarded. Given the choice, he preferred civil war, the potential destruction of the Roman *res publica*, and universal misery to suffering evil himself, the diminution of his standing, or an insult to his *dignitas*. This utterly clear-headed, historically well-documented (and eventually successful) narcissism on such a grand scale partly explains the fascination Caesar has exerted on successive generations.

We could say that Caesar chose to put his private interest before the common or public good;[19] that is, the ancients had a certain idealized conception of the way that holders of magistracies ought to make policy decisions. We share this conception. We believe (as the ancients did) that magistrates should, in making policy decisions, have as their goal the protection or advancement of the common good.[20] Analytically—and I wish to emphasize that this is *not* a historical claim—the most primitive notion of the common good is of some external state of affairs that members of a group would do well to bring about, such as building a dam or bridge, or instituting the regular worship of a certain god. Political arrangements and institutions can be seen as ways of organizing action so as to attain these external common goods. However, once we have established forms of common action, they can easily come to be seen as having some value of their own. This is not at all odd, because we might think that an important part of what we could reasonably mean by a "common good" is that there *be* reliable, established ways of organizing collective action. If we think that, in general, it is part of the common good to have such established, effective political structures, and we do not think the political institutions we have are too corrupt, we may even stretch our notion of the common good to encompass the preservation and maintenance of these political arrangements (*ceteris paribus*). This is part of the genuine rationale for political positions that are conservative or traditionalist and why it is not *merely* a confusion or political ideology to identify the common good with the status quo, that is, *res publica* in senses (b) and (d) above. Something can be said for connecting these two, provided one construes the status quo in a sufficiently general way to mean the mere fact that there are established ways of taking care of matters of common concern and pursuing the common good, and not to designate details of the existing political arrangements, particular policies, or the particular holders of office. No political arrangement known to us is perfect, and some are very far from being even morally tolerable. Obviously, the actual incumbent of an office will be strongly tempted to use the traditionalist argument to his or her own advantage, identifying him- or herself with the coherent stability of the existing arrangements. This argument can be misused, but that does not imply that it ought never to have any force at all.

Although, as I have mentioned, there was no "state" in the ancient world, many centuries later, when the state did come into existence, this last line of thought is one of the origins from which the doctrine "*raison d'état*" arose. If you *have* a state as your form of political organization, and especially if you are living in a world of competitive states, the preservation and flourishing of your state may be thought to give rise to an independent set of reasons for action.[21] If originally "public" means originally "pertaining to the concerns of all the people," and offices and magistracies are instituted to take care of these public concerns, then "public" can come to refer at least as directly to the offices as to the common concerns. "Public" can, then, come to mean something like "governmental" (although it cannot mean "state," as in "state-supported school" until the state exists). The public good can then slide from meaning "the common good of all, *including* the good of the government" (for instance, the conditions that allow the magistracies to function effectively) to meaning "the good of the government, including the common good of all" (where it is necessary to take account of it).

If the issue in 50–49 B.C. really is as starkly drawn as Caesar himself presents it—on the one hand, loss of status (*dignitas*) to him; on the other, evil to all humans—then it does not seem very problematic to identify the common good with the prevention of a civil war that will destroy the existing political order of the *res publica* and bring "evil to all humans" (even if the price that must be paid for that is a failure to recognize Caesar's unique merits). Caesar uses troops that have been entrusted to him as holder of a public magistracy in order to initiate a civil war in defense of his own status, and he does not even pretend that this is motivated by a desire to advance the common good or maintain the existing political structures. His *dignitas* is a property that he has independent, to some extent, of his public office. This is not to say that it would not be increased by his holding successive public offices—a Roman attained the *dignitas* of being a "consular" by virtue of having been elected to the consulship. Nevertheless Caesar came from an old patrician family and was a person of undoubted ability and accomplishment. His *dignitas* was neither a mere concomitant nor a mere result of holding public office; rather it was, to some extent, grounds for a claim to hold office. I take it that Caesar would proudly have insisted on this. Indeed, Caesar had to take drastic action in 50 B.C. because he had good reason to believe that his enemies intended to prosecute him as soon as they had the chance. Thus he needed to ensure for himself proleptically a high public office (the consulship) for 49 B.C. As consul he would have immunity from prosecution. The difficulty was that he could legally stand for office only if he left his troops and returned to Rome as a *priuatus*, thereby giving his enemies just the window of opportunity they needed. It was the Senate's refusal to allow him to ignore the usual rules and stand as a candidate in absentia that drove him to invade Italy. In this case, then, we say that he has allowed his private interest, that is, an interest he has as a non–office holder and one that is distinct from, and in this case directly contrary to, the common interest, inappropriately to influence a decision that ought to have been made based on what was best for the *res publica*.

Caesar's "private interest" in the maintenance of his *dignitas* and the recognition of his merits is not entirely the same thing as, for instance, simple financial corruption of the kind committed by a politician who uses his or her position for his or her own direct financial advantage. This is true partly because Caesar is appealing to merits that are themselves somewhat political—his past success and continuing capacity for success in advancing the interests of Rome. The relation between *dignitas* and public office in Rome was complicated, and it is tempting to think that part of the difficulty in getting clear about it is precisely because the concept of the state was lacking in Roman political thinking. Despite the Roman distinction between

office and incumbent, political power and its exercise in Rome was still "personal" in a way it ceases
to be when the concept of the state and the reality
of the modern state establish themselves. This perhaps makes it easier to understand how such a
thing as Caesar's career was possible, but still, in
this particular case, it is hard to think that Caesar
is acting "in the public interest." To believe this
one would have to think, for example, that he saw
the political bankruptcy of the late Roman *res publica* with complete clarity and consciously strove
to replace it with a charismatically based monar-
chy, so that his appeal to his own *dignitas* was an
appeal not exclusively or primarily to his "private"
interest but also to an interest in a beneficial revolutionary restructuring of the *res publica* around his
own person (such as later took place with Au-
gustus). This, however, would credit him not
merely with the highly developed jungle skills he
must have had to rise to the position of eminence
he occupied at the time of his assassination but also
with truly preternatural theoretical acumen.

Once a political order exists that assigns to certain people responsibility for taking care of matters
of common concern (i.e., "public affairs"), what
counts as a matter of "public concern" may well
expand. Whereas it might have originally denoted

external projects (building a new bridge), and then in addition the preservation and health of the arrangements for pursuing the common good, it can now reasonably be taken to include the reliability, competence, and general good character of those who present themselves as candidates for magistracies. In a world without a state structure or a police force, where obedience is problematic, it is also important to consider whether a candidate has enough "authority" to get himself obeyed effectively. In an unpredictable world, one kind of arrangement that can seem highly advantageous is to vest in the magistrates a discretionary power that allows them to react to unforeseen circumstances. It is then of the greatest importance to try to determine beforehand who would use such power competently, responsibly, and for the common good. It therefore becomes a matter of common concern what psychological traits and characteristics potential candidates for office have, and it is part of the common good that there be a sufficient number of appropriate candidates to fill all the available positions.

This is a different sense of public and private from the one we found in the case of Diogenes. The "public" in Diogenes' case is (1) a place to which everyone has free access, and thus where

everything that happens can be observed by anyone; and (2) a realm in which either inattention or
avoidance of disgusting or intimate behavior was
appropriate. "Public" in the case of Caesar does
not so much mean that to which anyone has access,
as (a) the realm of things that concern or affect
everyone, and then derivatively (b) the set of agencies that have *power over* (and responsibility for)
certain domains that are considered to concern everyone, that is, that concern "the common good."
The distinction between these senses of "public"
is highlighted when one observes that it is a highly
debatable, substantive claim, not a tautology, to as-
sert that everyone affected by certain decisions
should have even minimal cognitive access to those
decisions (i.e., that everything "public" in sense (a)
above is or should be "public" in sense (1) above).
As we know, the history of early Rome was marked
by a serious struggle about the publicity of the law
that applied to everyone. Only after a series of pro-
longed and often violent confrontations was the
principle established that the laws that applied to
all (and were in that sense "public") ought also to
be made known to all (displayed "in public"),
rather than being part of the secret knowledge of
the aristocratic holders of various priesthoods.
Even more highly debatable and substantive would

be the claim that everyone affected by a decision should be involved in any way in the control of the agencies who have power to set public policy. Finally, it would be an even stronger claim that what affected everyone should be decided on by everyone. It is by no means obvious that every "republic" must be a direct democracy.

CHAPTER IV

THE SPIRITUAL

AND THE

PRIVATE

WITH THAT we leave for the moment the sun-drenched world of successfully self-assertive Roman aristocrats and jolly Greek onanists to enter the steamy chiaroscuro regions of early Christianity.

In his *Confessions* (3.3.5) the African rhetorician Aurelius Augustinus reports that he once attempted to initiate a sexual relationship with a young woman whom he saw and lusted after in a church while religious ceremonies were being conducted. He does not describe what went on in any detail, except to say that God "beat" him "with heavy punishments" because of it, which presumably means either that he suffered from the remorse of a guilty conscience, was afflicted with a venereal disease, or perhaps just felt the continuing lash of lust. There is no implication that he had any actual physical contact with the woman in the church, and, in fact, we can be pretty sure that if he had been able to copulate with her in the church or elsewhere he would have made very sure that they were completely unobserved. In *The City of God* (14.20) he denies that the stories about Cynics copulating in public could be true,[1] claiming that it is so unimaginable that anyone could conceivably have sexual pleasure with lots of people thronging around watching (*"humano premente conspectu"*) that one must assume that the story is false. One might think of this as an early application of the Davidsonian principle of charity, which gives unintentional testimony to Augustine's own great personal innocence, and perhaps also to a certain lack of imagination on his part. In any case, he suggests that the story arose because the Cynics, for philosophical reasons, shammed intercourse in public, and no one was standing close enough actually to see what was going on under the long philosopher's cloaks they affected. Anyone who actually *practiced* what the Cynics preached could expect, Augustine claims, to be covered with the saliva of people who would gather around to spit on them (*"certe conspuentium salivis obruerentur"*). Augustine seems to assume that spitting on people would be perfectly natural under the circumstances, something that does not require special comment and is clearly not as bad as concupiscence.

In the mid-380s A.D. Augustine began to feel oppressed by various social and professional obligations and pressures. He had moved from Carthage first to Rome and then to one of the administrative centers of the late Roman world, Milan, and embarked on a highly successful but taxing career as teacher of rhetoric. To be a teacher of rhetoric in the late ancient world was to exercise a profession that required the continual demonstration of a variety of highly disciplined competences in conditions of high visibility, that is, in an extremely public context (in both senses of "public," that which emerged from the analysis of Diogenes' behavior and that which emerged from the account of Caesar's action). In addition, his mother, the redoubtable Monica, had just forced him to send his long-term mistress (and mother of his son) back to Africa as part of a plan to secure for him a fashionable arranged marriage. Finally, he continued to be plagued by various religious doubts and scruples. As a response to this situation, Augustine decided to withdraw from "the world," from the business of teaching rhetoric, to an isolated villa in Cassiciacum with a few close friends for spiritual meditation. This was an extremely important step in a series of conversion experiences that brought him eventually to embrace Catholic Christianity.[2] An important part of this process was his eventual realization that God might be construed to be incorporeal. As he withdrew physically from the "world" into the literary and philosophical refuge of Cassiciacum, so in book 10 he describes retreating into himself, into the halls of his memory to reflect on the nature of his relation to God,[3] although it is also perhaps relevant to remember that his withdrawal in Cassiciacum was *not* into strictly anchorite isolation but was the undertaking of a group of friends who decided to devote themselves *collectively* to philosophical and religious discussion.

A major part of the task Augustine set himself in *Confessions* is to know himself. The self-knowledge to which he aspires, however, although it may seem on the surface to have strong similarities with earlier (Socratic) and later (Cartesian) kinds, actually has a rather different structure. The "self" he wishes to come to know is not that of the (potential) artisan who has mastered the craft of living or the self that is revealed in minimal reflection—the *sum* implicit in each *cogito* or the "I think" that must be able to accompany all my representations—but his state of will, desire, and love. If for Socrates I should be an unrelenting searcher for

the general definitions of the virtues that will allow
me to lead a good life, and if for Descartes I am a
thinking substance, for Augustine I am a tempo-
rally shifting structure of desire, or I am the history
of my loves. To come to the appropriate form of
knowledge of who I am requires that I not merely
have keen cognitive faculties and deploy them persistently and correctly, but also that I have the appropriate psychological disposition and be in the
proper state of desire/love. Self-knowledge is a
kind of reflective desire, a desire turned back on
the history of my past forms of desire. I can know
myself only if I (properly) love myself, but loving
oneself properly turns out to be a complicated, un-
ending task. It further turns out that in order for
the desirous reflection, which is the main mechanism of self-knowledge, to be successful, it cannot
be solitary (à la Descartes) or conversationally dia-
lectical with other human partners (à la Socrates)
but must take the form of a kind of conversation
with an extra-human entity (God),[4] a conversation
like that instantiated in *Confessions*. God is correctly understood as (a) ideally and fully benevolent, (b) ineluctably exigent in that he holds us to
conformity with extremely demanding moral injunctions, (c) omniscient, and (d) the Creator of us
and the whole universe, who is therefore a principle of reality.[5] To love ourselves properly requires

seeing ourselves as we really are but that means
seeing ourselves from God's point of view, because
reality is simply what God sees from his point of
view. For me to be able to see even partially from
God's perspective requires, however, that I ante-
cedently love him. Thus the form of desirous cog-
nition that I direct at myself, if it is to have a
chance of being successful, must be informed by a
prior love of God. Only if I love that other, God,
can I know myself in the appropriate sense. Finally,
the conversation is *not* supposed to be a Rortyean
swapping of favorite metaphors in conditions of
ἐποχή with no political consequences; rather, it is
supposed to be emotionally and practically transformative, to cause me to change my state of desire
radically, through adopting God as a unique object
of love, knowing him (and thus what he requires
of me) more fully and correctly, following his cate-
gorical injunctions, and thus acting differently in
the world, although the "difference" this makes
will, like all human phenomena, be radically ambiguous and not necessarily clearly visible to other
humans. As our soul conforms more and more to
God's injunctions, we are able to see more and
more of ourselves more and more clearly from that
point of view, and thus more and more correctly.
To have a spiritual life is to be a historically extended process of reconstructing the whole of

one's personality, including not merely its cognitive aspects but especially its states of desire in the
context of an extended (imaginary) dialogue with
God. This is a rather different model from that
which one finds in Socrates or Descartes, a different model not just in terms of the object of self-
knowledge, but also of what it is to know.[6]

In book 10, in any case, Augustine claims that it
is in memory and reflection that he will encounter
himself among the images of all he has experienced. The most important aspects of ourselves,
he claims, are not the corporeal ones but our inner
state, the state of our souls relative to God. This
state is completely hidden from other human beings, inaccessible to them, knowable only to ourselves and to God.

To be more exact, our inner state is fully knowable to God and partly knowable to ourselves,
knowable to ourselves in fact only with difficulty[7]
and only to the extent to which we stand in the
right relation to God. In a sense, we each have
privileged but not direct or incorrigible access to
ourselves because we have an access no other
human being can have, but to make use of it in
such a way as to come to a correct understanding
of ourselves we must go through God, and, try as
we will, we will never in this life succeed in assimi-
lating God's point of view fully, and so we will

never be fully transparent to ourselves. To adopt a terminology used by Kierkegaard: one never *is* a Christian, one can at best be *becoming* a Christian.[8]

To put parts of this view slightly more pedantically in the technical language of contemporary philosophy, Augustine holds a number of theses. First, there are inner states to which we have privileged epistemic access in the sense that others cannot know them as well or in the same way as we can know them ourselves. Second, the privileged access we have is neither a form of incorrigible nor of easy access, and in fact it is an important constituent of Augustine's position that our cognitive access to ourselves is highly fallible and extremely difficult, and that we will never be fully transparent to ourselves. Third, the strictly cognitive and the emotive/desirous are, at least in the case of any human self-knowledge worth the name, inextricably connected. In particular, one cannot have correct self-knowledge (especially of such things as states of desire, motives, etc.) without being oneself in an appropriate state of desire. Fourth, correct self-knowledge cannot be obtained through solitary reflection but only through dialogue with God. This thesis takes one up to the very limits of comprehensible reconstruction of this position for a modern atheist like me. On the one hand, one could say that Augustine *really* re-

jects the whole notion that there could be radically
private self-knowledge, because correct self-
knowledge for him is attainable only in dialogue
with another person (albeit a nonhuman person);
then one could go on to locate his position in the
historical line that leads through Hegel to Buber
and Habermas. On the other hand, since I think
that "God" designates an imaginary entity, one
could equally say that obviously all that is really
necessary is that one be capable of constructing
such an imaginary Other from whose point of view
one can view the self. There might be social conditions, such as the acquisition of a language, that
are necessary for this to be possible, but once those
general conditions are satisfied the process itself
could take place with no one else (i.e., no other
human being) present and "in private."[9] The fifth
thesis I wish to ascribe to Augustine is that such
inner states, particularly the state of the will, are
terribly important, are highly, in fact infinitely, valuable, are definitive of who we are, and are, or
ought to be, the final object of "moral" evaluation
(understanding "moral" in a wide sense). We are
to be judged, that is, not by what we do but by the
state of our wills.

Christian salvation would seem to be the private
good par excellence, and the spiritual life is its
mechanism, but the Christian must also act on di-

vine injunctions in this world, and these injunctions will not be merely those given to us by natural human reason. The way Christians act should,
therefore, differ from the way pagans do.[10] The
City of God and the City of Man coexist here on
earth, but, although they differ *toto caelo*, no one
can be sure who belongs to which.[11]

Despite the emphasis on the "interiority" of
human religious experience which, in Augustine's
view, is constitutive of it, this approach is highly
materialistic in another sense, at least to the extent
of taking the external physical circumstances in
which an act is performed into account in evaluating it. Augustine is highly exercised by the question of whether women who are raped should be
considered to be polluted by lust, and answers this
in the negative (provided they have not given inner
consent: *"sine ulla sua consensione"*).[12] Similarly, if
one wished to judge Augustine morally, one ought
to judge his internal state, but it is also important
that the act of lusting described in *Confessions*
(3.3.5) took place "within the walls of the church."
The full proper answer to Victorinus' rhetorical
question (*Confessiones* 8.2), "So the walls, then,
make the Christian?" (*"Ergo parietes faciunt Chris-
tianos?"*), is, despite Augustine's emphasis on the
inner life, yes.

The account of spirituality I have given has two notable features. First, spirituality is connected with some notion of discipline. As Hegel correctly noted,[13] "spirit" is not a natural category; one *is* not spirit, but *becomes* spirit, and that usually means one *makes oneself* or *turns oneself into* spirit by the use of some techniques. The second notable feature is that many forms of spirituality are distinctly related to the phenomenon of disgust. I will mention three different attitudes. I will assume, following my discussion above, that despite the culturally specific differences that can be found among the *objects*, the reaction of disgust, as a biologically based impulse to reject certain qualitatively specified substances, is, in one form or another, sufficiently widespread in human societies to count as what we would call "natural." One has the usual problem of potential historical anachronism when speaking of the forms of "spirituality" of pre- and non-Christian cultures. I will assume that the Christian conception contains two components: (a) something about the relation to a metaphysically fundamental reality that is transcendent (that, if it is construed as personal, can be called "God"); and (b) some notion of human self-fashioning in the "inner" realm of "private" thoughts and desires to attain a proper relation to that reality. Where we find historical sequences that lead in the direction of a possible conjunction between some form of these two features, we can reasonably speak of spirituality.[14]

The first form of spirituality is one that arises out of primitive notions connected with purity, that the god or gods must be approached only by unblemished, physically healthy people with clean clothing and unsullied hands. This is presumably a projection of human affects on to the god. Just as we do not wish the king to react to our approach with disgust—he may then turn down our petition—so we do not wish the god to turn away in disgust from our sacrifice. The idea of purity can gradually be extended metaphorically from the physical to the moral sphere: the mysteries exclude first pockmarked shepherds in greasy smocks with disgustingly filthy hands, but then also homicides who may not literally have hands stained red with human blood but are still "marked" by the blood they have shed in some way invisible to the human eye. Finally, even "liars," tax collectors, "developers," and other unsavory and unrighteous types might be excluded, even if they have no physical deformity or disgusting skin condition.

The second possible form is one I will call "ideally indifferentist," which implies a form of complete and radical self-control. If what is most important is the cultivation of an internal state that puts one into or allows one to adopt the right attitude toward a transcendent reality—God, the One, and so on—then it is possible to see all reactions of disgust directed at objects in this world as irrational, ungrounded, and unwarranted. No bit of matter is any farther from spiritual reality than any other, because (for instance) one might think that *all* matter is infinitely far. So one cultivates indifference and attempts to ignore or do away with one's feelings of disgust. An ideal state would be one in which such feelings did not exist. This is *not* the same as the view of Diogenes of Sinope, although certain early Christians noted some strong elective affinities between Cynism and Christianity, notably the rejection of convention, of the civic and political world and its honor-culture, and so on. Nevertheless, Diogenes' view seems to have been a radically naturalistic one, not a protoform of spirituality.[15] This is true despite the fact that Diogenes, like Socrates, was said to have been the recipient of an oracle that gave him the characteristically ambiguous advice "παραχάραττειν τὸ νόμισμα," which might literally be taken to mean "change the imprint on the currency" but also "change the existing moral valuations." The story ran that Diogenes first tried out the life of a moneyer, abasing the local currency, until, getting into trouble for this, he realized that the god was instructing him to lead a life according to nature. Diogenes' life of shamelessness was, like Socrates', an attempt to do what the god commanded. The "god" here may be a reliable, although teasingly obscure, source of information, but he is certainly not the creator and transcendent principle of reality in anything like the Christian sense, and so, to put it as an oxymoron, he is himself part of the "natural" order.

Some of the similarities between Diogenes of Sinope and Nietzsche are striking.[16] "*Umwertung aller Werte*" (the "transvaluation of all values"), the phrase Nietzsche uses to characterize the project that occupied him during the last few years of productive life, is a virtual translation of "παρα-χάραττειν τὸ νόμισμα." Nietzsche, too, has a radically naturalist position with no place for any form of "spirituality." Thus one ideal one finds in Nietzsche is that of a person who has what Nietzsche calls his or her own "*pro*" and "*contra*" fully under his or her control.[17] Since disgust is a form of bodily *contra*, this ideal would presumably imply a full control over my own experience of disgust. Two qualifications are needed here, though. First, although Nietzsche is a naturalist in that he rejects all transcendent entities, he differs from Diogenes in that for him there is *no* model, no normative

principle of reality, not even "nature." Second, the
ideal of having one's *pro* and *contra* completely
in one's control is not one that humans can even
hope to attain—as humans we will always be potentially subject to overpowering waves of disgust
(or, for that matter, admiration) that will, to some
extent, do with us what they will. What Nietzsche
calls the "*Übermensch*" is the idea of someone who
could realize the ideal of self-control, but the
Übermensch is by definition not human. Interest-
ingly enough, Augustine has an account of a state
like this in which features of our somatic constitution that are now recalcitrant would be fully under
our conscious voluntative control. He thinks that
this is the state in which humans lived before the
Fall from Grace. Given Augustine's own obses-
sions, he is most interested in whether a pre-laps-
arian man would be fully in control of his own
erection.[18] Before original sin, he thinks, Adam
could summon up an erection at any time by an
act of pure volition and never experience one save
as a result of such a volition. For Augustine, that
is, nonvoluntary erections are a sign of the fallen
and corrupted state of the human will. For
Nietzsche, that our own reactions of disgust are *in
fact* not fully under our control is merely a sign that
we are human, that is, a sign of our natural human
state of weakness.

The third form of spirituality is that of a specifically Christian spirituality that insists seriously
on the all-redeeming power of love and encour-
ages an extension of that love even to objects of
disgust.[19] Thus Kolnai, at the end of his essay on
disgust, cites and analyzes a poem by Franz Werfel
that describes Jesus' confrontation with a heap of
moles, worms, carrion, and all the most disgusting
forms of teeming animal life and his eventual embrace of them all, and celebrates this as a triumph
of the power of divine love.[20] As Kolnai points out,
this form of "overcoming of disgust" is very different from two others it might seem to resemble.
First, there is precivilized apathy, that is, the case
of someone who, for whatever reason, simply fails
to develop the usual reactions of somatic negation,
including reactions of disgust. Second, there are
those who, through exercise or habit, become in-
ured to what would otherwise seem disgusting:
thus many in the medical profession eventually fail
to experience what would otherwise seem to be
fairly widespread reactions of disgust. Neither of
these two forms of overcoming disgust is a good
model for the Christian spirituality noted here. If
the point of Christianity is that it indicates the
overwhelming *power* of love, then that power can
be demonstrated only by acting on and van-
quishing something that is itself recognized as ex-

tremely powerful and deep-rooted. The Christian is not supposed to become like a surgeon or like an *enfant sauvage* but is to feel the usual reactions of disgust as keenly as anyone else does, *and yet* overcome them. For this purpose, the more disgusting the object or activity, the better. This explains some of those acts Max Weber calls the "extraordinary instances of charity" (*"karitative Virtuosenleistungen"*) by medieval saints.[21]

The "interior" phenomena Augustine is analyzing are ones we have come to describe with the terminology of *privacy*. Augustine himself, however, would have been unlikely to describe them in this way, if only because *priuatus*, as we have seen, already had an established usage in Latin (non–office holder), and also because, in a sense, one of the things he learns is precisely that he is never alone but always within earshot of God, and God's ears are sharp enough to detect even the tiniest rustle of an inchoate velleity. Still, we would say that our states of mind, both cognitive and desirous, are "private"—we have access to them that no other human being has. This sense of "private" is different from the first two. My mental states are supposed to be epistemically *inherently* private (and they are then construed as ontologically private), whereas Diogenes' choice of a private or public place to masturbate or defecate is a choice between two places that have the same ontological status, and whatever difference there may be in their epistemic status is merely accidental and contextual—what you cannot see from your standpoint, I may be able to see from mine. The "private" in the case of Diogenes is an invisible place to which *he* should withdraw so as not to offend others; in Augustine's case, "the private" is in its origin a domain to which he wishes to withdraw when social demands become too oppressive, the villa at Cassiciacum, and eventually an ontologically privileged place of withdrawal within his own mind.[22] Similarly, Caesar's *dignitas*, which is the content of his "private" interest (i.e., an interest in conflict with the common good), is preeminently something that is *not* private in the sense of Augustinean interiority. A basic property of Caesar's *dignitas* is that other people experience it. It must be an external part of the social world; other people must treat him in a certain way; his *dignitas* must be as real for them as it is for him.

The Christian spirituality to which Augustine aspires does not require that one be a *priuatus* in the sense of a non–office holder; in principle, kings can be members of the City of God, and, after all, a bishop is a kind of office holder of the "*populus Christianus*," an officer of the Church Militant. Augustine himself did not want episcopal responsibil-

ities, but he did not think they were strictly incompatible with leading a life of the spirit. Similarly,
the spiritual life does not require physical inacces-
sibility in a place where one can be neither seen
nor heard (nor smelled). Ambrose, we are given to
think, reads the Scriptures silently because he is
constantly surrounded by people, even when reading, and does not wish to have to explain difficult
passages to random passersby.[23] What it does require is capacity to focus one's attention on one's
own state of desire and its relation to God, and
this process is one that will be cognitively almost
completely inaccessible to other human beings and
only partially accessible to the person performing
the reflection, although it will always be fully
transparent to God.[24]

I have distinguished a number of senses of the
public/private distinction that arise in three different contexts. First is the idea that some things (especially features of ourselves or actions) might be
offensive to others, and we should therefore try to
keep these to ourselves and not thrust them on
others' notice without their consent; they are "private" (we say) and should not be made public or
done in public. Second are the goals or policies the
pursuit of which will differentially benefit some
particular individual or group to the detriment of
the clear interest of the relevant members of the

universe of discourse as a whole.[25] If we think we can make this distinction, we speak of the common or the public interest and contrast it with what we will call the "private" interest of the individual or subgroup in question. Third are the various ontological and epistemological senses of "private" developed in the course of working out the Augustinian model of philosophical reflection, although increasingly, as time goes on, Augustine's rich conception of self-relating forms of desire, mediated through conversation with an idealized Other as the matrix for self-knowledge, comes to be replaced by a more austere and more strictly cognitivist model of self-knowledge.

CHAPTER V

LIBERALISM

The Augustinian emphasis on the inner, spiritual life was highly influential and contributed much to our modern assumption that the realm of our own thoughts, beliefs, impulses, and desires, and perhaps also the realm of communication, should be of special concern to us, but there is no direct line of descent from his doctrine to characteristic liberal views, particularly to anti-paternalism. For Augustine, there *was* a father in the form of his God, and various social institutions could, in principle, wield the paternal rod legitimately. To put this more concretely, Augustine's legacy was twofold: on the one hand, he affirmed the infinite value of the individual inner life, but, on the other, by calling on the secular powers to impose religious uniformity by force (during the Donatist controversy), and by writing to justify this intervention, he became the patron saint of religious persecution—the "first theorist of the Inquisition."[1]

Liberalism is concerned with the public/private distinction primarily because of an interest in defending what it calls "the private sphere" or "the private realm" not just from religious inquisition but from all kinds of intrusion. None of the senses of "the private" mentioned in the previous sections, however, is really identical with the sense of "private" that plays a role in *that* part of liberal political theory which devotes itself to the protection of "the private sphere." Since this is the case, or so I will claim, taking any of the above three kinds of distinction as the model for a *general* distinction between public and private (or for *the* distinction as it is found in the writings of liberals) is a mistake. Thus good liberals all think that my bank balance is my "private" concern, no one else's business, and that its confidentiality is to be protected; people in general—that is, "any comer" or "anyone who happens to want to know"—ought not to have automatic access to it, either cognitive or real access. That my financial situation is my own private concern does not mean that I ought to keep it to myself because anyone would be disgusted to be confronted with it—in my own case that might well be true, but it is probably not true as a general rule—nor does it mean that the state of my bank account is ontologically or epistemically private. If some feature of my life really is ontologically pri-

vate, it is pointless to try to protect it from possible
surveillance. One might think that it is "private"
in the sense the term figures in the discussion of
Caesar's crossing of the Rubicon. "Private" here
means, however, "what *ought not* (for whatever reason) to be interfered with either by other individuals or by social and political institutions or agencies." The point of distinguishing between public
and private in the case of Caesar, though, was to
determine whether something—some private interest—had interfered with the pursuit of the public good (and the almost unavoidable conclusion in
Caesar's case was that it had). "What ought not to
be interfered with" is, however, not the same
thing, extensionally or intensionally, as "what
ought not to interfere." Although they are not the
same thing, however, perhaps they are, as it were,
two sides of the same distinction.[2] The "private"
things that ought not to influence Caesar's decision as a magistrate, allowing for the obvious historical changes that have expanded the range of
"private" things,[3] are, in principle, exactly the kind
of things that ought not to be interfered with by a
liberal government, and vice versa. Financial gain
to himself ought not to have influenced Caesar's
decisions, and a liberal government ought not to
interfere in his financial transactions. If this were
true, then perhaps, after all, there would be one

central distinction between private and public operating here in the political realm. Perhaps this is
right in some rather abstract sense, but still it
seems to me to overlook the actual logic of the way
the distinction is made and deployed in the two
cases. Thus, although Caesar would not be acting
to ensure the "public good" if he did something
in his capacity as a magistrate that would benefit
himself financially but would disadvantage Rome
(whatever exactly "Rome" would be taken to mean
in this context), his financial situation was *not* his
"private affair" in anything like the sense assumed
by modern liberals. Political rights of various kinds
in Rome were explicitly dependent on property
qualifications. So, for instance, any senator who
fell below a certain level of wealth could be excluded from the Senate by the censors. One's financial situation was therefore a matter of public
concern and public scrutiny. In addition, there are
also "things" that ought not to interfere with Caesar's decisions as a magistrate that would *not* be
part of the protected private sphere of liberalism.
A magistrate may run a criminal operation on the
side and exercise his magistral powers to bring
some extra business its way, but such an operation
would not be covered by liberal forms of protection of the private sphere. On the other hand, one
thing that is emphatically in the liberal "private

sphere" of "things" to be protected is my beliefs
and opinions, including my political opinions, and
thus also presumably my conception of the common or public good. Assuming a Western European– or North American–style parliamentary democracy, is a politician never supposed to act on
his or her "private" conception of the common
good? Is that even conceivably possible? Is doing
so promoting a "private" interest? Or does this
"private" conception suddenly become a "public"
one when the politician is elected or appointed?
Perhaps this distinction can be maintained when
applied to certain judges or low-level administra-
tors who, in routine cases, are thought to need to
do nothing but "follow the rules." The judge may
impose the death penalty that the law requires, despite objecting "privately," for instance on moral
grounds, to capital punishment or even thinking
that capital punishment is not "in the common interest," although it may be difficult enough to say
what it is "merely to follow the rules" in cases of
any complexity. Nevertheless, this seems a completely inappropriate model of politics. In real politics candidates rarely have a chance to expound
their "conception of the good" in any but the most
ludicrously general or risibly specific terms; elec-
tors are ignorant of the various programs anyway,
and once elections are over (at the latest) politics

is about compromise, alliance formation, party discipline, and effective strategy, as well as about dealing with *unforeseen* circumstances. Is it a demand
of the pursuit of the public good that one block
out the whole reality of politics?

So the question of what the "private" is for liberalism is the question of what sorts of things, that
is, what kinds of goods, it is desirable or advisable
to protect from what kind of social and governmental interferences for what reasons and in what
ways. The question about how the private is to be
distinguished, and protected, from the public
transforms itself for liberalism into four further
questions:

(a) What kind of and how extensive a
sphere is it advisable to have that is defended
from encroachment by "the public"?

(b) What is meant by "the public" in (a):
does it mean only the government, or does it
include more general social institutions, practices, public opinion?

(c) For what reason is it advisable to defend
the private sphere (as defined above) from
"the public" (as defined above)?

(d) How is the defense to be enforced (e.g.,
through legal means, economic means, etc.)?

Two thinkers whose views clearly illustrate the general liberal approach to the public and the private are J. S. Mill and John Dewey. Mill, to take his views first, strongly suggests a certain way of looking at public/private as a distinction of types of action.[4] A private action is one that "affects only the agent"; a public one is an action that also affects others. Mill seems to think it of primary importance to get this distinction right. Does Mill get it right? Did Diogenes' action in the Athenian marketplace affect only himself or also other people? Is it public or private?

In the case of particular interest to Mill, that of religious belief, he thinks that one must first properly see that religious *belief* is a private matter, because the action of believing affects only the agent. Then one can see that such religious belief belongs in the private sphere. Finally, one concludes that that which is thus private should be protected. Mill thinks that the private sphere should not be interfered with by either government or social pressure. The difficulty, as has often been pointed out, is that "affect" is too hopelessly vague a term to provide the basis for a good theory. If your belief is really something that is strictly or epistemically private, and thus that I can know nothing about, it needs no protection. In addition, it is in the nature of most religious beliefs that they are supposed to affect not just the believer but also others, because the believer is supposed to act on them in the world. Finally, even your religious belief may well affect me to the extent that I can or do know about it—for instance, you may hold beliefs I find repellent or I myself may think that God will hold all those who live in a certain society responsible for homogeneous conformity of "true" belief in that society. Perhaps it is none of my business—after all, these are *their* ontologically private opinions— but surely it does affect me if all my neighbors are fantasizing about me in a certain way, for instance, as an "infidel" who must (eventually, when the time comes and the balance of power shifts) be given the choice between conversion and extermination, *even if their behavior toward me is irreproachable at the present moment.* What Mill really means is that "affect" should be given a certain reading— what "affects" me in this sense is what could "harm or injure me materially" or "have a deleterious effect on my interests." Then my religious beliefs do not affect you *unless you have a very particular theory,* namely, the view that God will punish collectively communities that allow persons to hold the wrong religious views. Such beliefs are widespread in pre-liberal societies. In Europe up to the eighteenth century the holding of heretical beliefs was one of *the* public crimes par excellence "through which the whole republic, city, or other community is harmed";[5] the suppression of heresy was therefore in *everyone's* interest. Liberals, however, think that theory (of collective responsibility before God) is wrong and disallow that you are "affecting" your neighbors and fellow citizens in any relevant sense simply by holding a certain belief, even a heretical one. So the liberal can make an effective distinction between public and private in cases like this by first determining who is "affected" by a given action where "affect" means "(potentially) injures materially" or "harms the interests of," and then by evaluating the truth or falsity of the theory the agents in question hold about what harms or might harm their interests. The question is then: who does the evaluating? Liberals, of course, think they ought to have the final word, although they are generally careful to camouflage this as well as they can. In other words, it is the fact that liberals *think* that the beliefs of religiously minded persons (e.g., that God will hold *all* responsible for the heresies of any one member of the society) are false that is supposed to count as a reason for thinking that religious people have no grounds for the claim that heresy causes real "harm." It is not clear, however, why this whole line of argument is saying anything more than this: if you have the views about reasonable belief and action that liberals prefer, you will also endorse their policy proposals. This circular system of self-reinforcing beliefs seems hardly worth stating. To be sure, it is not irrelevant that this portion of liberalism *is* thus self-reinforcing (if it is), because many belief systems, or systems of beliefs together with policy recommendations, are not self-reinforcing but self-defeating or self-undermining. Thus some, notably Daniel Bell, have thought that capitalism was a self-contradicting social, cultural, and economic system.[6] If this is *not* true of some form of liberalism, this would not be irrelevant but would mean that that form of liberalism was at least a live candidate for discussion.[7]

The twentieth-century philosopher most concerned with the distinction between the public and private was John Dewey, and one can hardly improve on his account of the central intuition that lies behind the most enlightened liberal usage of these terms:[8]

When the consequences of an action are confined, or are thought to be confined mainly to the persons directly engaged in it, the transaction is a private one. . . . Yet if it is found that the consequences . . . extend beyond [those] directly concerned . . . the act acquires a public capacity. . . . The line between private and public is to be drawn on the basis of the extent and scope of the consequences of acts which are so important as to need control, whether by inhibition or promotion. The public consists of all those who are affected by the indirect consequences of transactions to such an extent that it is deemed necessary to have these consequences systematically cared for.[9]

The distinction between public and private, then, is a relative one in a number of distinct senses: first, it depends on the level of social knowledge of the possible consequences of acts. Second, it depends on what we allow or disallow to count as "consequences" of action. Third, it also depends on the value judgments of the members of the society and thus on their views and decisions about what consequences "need" to be controlled. Finally, it depends on an initial decision about who is considered to be "directly concerned." How do we know that the local priest, bishop, or commissar is not automatically "directly concerned" in every transaction?

Note, too, that this is a self-describedly liberal account but one in which "public/private" does not function as the origin of some kind of legitimatory claim. It is not that we discover what the distinction is between the public and private and then proceed to determine what value attitudes we should have to it, but rather that given our values and knowledge we decide what sorts of things we think need regulating or caring for—and then stamp them "public." One of the things we may think needs collective caring for is individuality, and so we may set out to organize society so that certain acts are excluded from closer regulation. The "private," then, is that socially and legally protected residual domain.

One subdivision of the category of the "private" is of particular interest and concern to contemporary liberalism, and that is "privacy." If "private," in general, carries with it the idea of privilege, "private property" is property over which some individual has privileged control independent of occupying some (public) political office, and the central part of the idea of "privacy" is limited or restricted or privileged *cognitive* access. One way to think of the origin of the idea that privacy is a great human value is to see it in connection with the growth of conceptions of "public opinion."

"Public opinion" is a concept that originates in the eighteenth century, and its development quickly comes to stand under the shadow of the assumption that such public opinion can be a potent social and political force.[10] However, "public opinion" designates a normatively ambiguous phenomenon. On the one hand, two positive hopes are associated with it: the hope that it can be mobilized as a brake on forms of irrational, self-serving, inhumane, and despotic power, and to protect "the public" against maladministration and miscarriages of justice, and the more general hope that it can be harnessed as a far-reaching force for civilizing manners and tastes, and that public discussion may promote tolerance—a highly praised virtue—and contribute to the formation of rational political goals and policies. So on the positive side is the demand for maximal publicity on the part of governments and "public" administration, and a celebration of a robust "public realm" in which public opinion can be formed and exert its salutary influence.[11] On the other hand, though, some theorists become aware of the potential of "public opinion" for enforcing social conformity and repressing individuals.[12] This leads to calls to defend the individual from its pressure. Since the force of public opinion is, in the first instance, a force of mere opinion, it would seem to be adequate and appropriate to guard against it by restricting access people might have to experiences or information about certain disagreeable kinds of things, for instance, offensive beliefs or forms of behavior, which could be the basis for forming a negative opinion about a certain person or group.

For the liberal to say that the government should respect my "privacy" means that there is a sphere or area within which physical or cognitive access to me should not be allowed to others not of my choosing. Why would we want to protect such a sphere? Why should it be thought to be important? There are several possible reasons. First, in societies in which certain kinds of competitive structures exist, I can have an interest in preventing interference with my ability to compete, and with preventing access to knowledge about me that can be of use to my competitors. Thus, if I am bidding against an economic rival, it might make a big difference to me whether I was able to keep the actual state of my finances (and the nature and extent of my other economic projects) "secret." The members of some given society, then, might think that certain competitive structures had distinct advantages, for instance, that a competitive market was especially efficient. The members of that society might also think that certain forms of privacy had to be maintained and protected if the valued structure in question was to survive and flourish. This would be a reason for trying to enforce the appropriate forms of privacy.

Second there can be interactions, for instance, in which two or more persons focus their attention on something delicate which they are doing jointly, and in which the presence of other persons would be a disturbance or a distraction. The cases that immediately spring to mind are those in which the physical presence of another is disturbing, for instance, when acrobats or musicians are practicing working together or when surgeons are performing a complex and delicate procedure. In these cases there is nothing to be ashamed of; that is not the grounds for insisting that no one else have access to the practice space or the operating room. It is just that humans have limited and sometimes fragile powers of attention, and for many it imposes a further burden to concentrate on one thing while blocking out something else. Humans are so constituted that we usually pay some attention to what other people in our immediate surroundings are doing—this is why the principle of disattendability, which I discussed earlier, is needed—so in situations in which we think we need to concentrate our attention completely on some job at hand, it makes sense to ensure that no other persons are in our immediate environment. Extraneous humans in this context would count as one kind of disturbance, but there are others. It could be that two or more people are engaged in something they are ashamed of, although it might in no sense be illegal or even immoral. Sexual examples spring to mind. The presence of others, or even others' indirect cognitive access to their action (through infrared telescopy, the use of long-distance audio receivers, etc.), might then reasonably count as a disturbance because it might cause feelings of inhibition. One can then try to extend this argument from cases of interaction to cases of solitary activities. Thus Augustine might have thought that the presence of another would distract him from concentrating on confessing to God, but apparently Ambrose did not, and some people, although not Diogenes of Sinope, might be inhibited from masturbating by the presence of others. From the fact that someone *claims* that the presence of others is distracting, it does not follow that that claim must be accepted. Thus we would not generally accept a claim made by someone traveling by train that the mere physical presence of another person in the next seat would be a disturbance. If, then, we think that a certain kind of activity is valuable, and we think that some mode of real or cognitive access should legitimately count as a disturbance, we may think that the activity should be surrounded by protective barriers.

A third possible reason for wanting to protect a private sphere is that I might think there should be a sphere in which I am free to carry out experiments. I might hold this view because I think it is good for society as a whole that such experimentation take place, or I could highly value individual self-development and self-realization and think it essential for such self-development that experimentation be possible (or both). Since it is in the nature of experiments sometimes to fail, I could think it socially important to protect people from the full consequences of failure; to be more exact, to prevent others from knowing about that failure. Further, one category of the private is the intimate, and many theorists have thought that there are forms of self-affirmation that humans need and can develop only if they stand in appropriate relations of intimacy to others; these are constituents of the good human life.[13]

It is not self-evidently the case that the best way to foster human individuation and self-development, assuming we accept these Romantic goals, is to ensure complete privacy, either protection of a sphere of activity in which action is not interfered with *or* protection of a sphere of action to which no one has epistemic access (without the permission of the agents involved).[14] It is an odd property of this question that one cannot even be sure whether it is an empirical one, probably because the concepts of "self-development," "interference," and so on, are not sufficiently clear and sufficiently independent of one another for us to be able to imagine any way to test claims in this area that would not be at least potentially circular.

The liberal ideal of antipaternalism arose with Humboldt from a naturalistic theory of the value of self-development and a naive empirical assumption that self-development and state activity were inversely related.[15] Later versions have become in some ways more sophisticated and less open to empirical confutation. Thus one can give up the idea that the human good is self-development and activity, and claim that only the given individual can say in what his or her good consists and that there are few limits on what this can be—for a given individual it might well consist, as Friedrich Schlegel suggested,[16] in a state not of high entelechy but of "divine vegetation." Since no other person or agency can know better than I do in what my good consists, no such external agency can legitimately interfere in my action against my will in the name of promoting my good.[17] Certain versions of the liberal ideal of antipaternalism, especially some derived from the Kantian tradition,[18] presuppose a standard of social (and moral) self-sufficiency for human individuals that is impossibly high.[19]

It might well be the case that the liberal ideal of an individual subjectivity that has parts of itself barricaded off against all others should yield to an

ideal derived from, or at least open to, the influence of the third of the French revolutionary slo-
gans: fraternity.[20] Many people have found it an at-
tractive ideal to imagine a society where the
barriers were lower, more flexible and permeable,
less regulated by legal codes, and less strictly or
less uniformly enforced by coercive agencies of
government. Even if the above claim is true, that
self-realization requires a sphere within which one
can experiment and fail, it might not obviously follow that individuals must be protected from the
social consequences of perceived failure. Why not
change social attitudes so that failure has no
stigma, rather than building up barriers of privacy?
Why not learn to accept failure and dependence?
The liberal thinks that such social change is impos-
sible, and that the goal of overcoming disgust and
shame is a perfectionist or utopian one; perhaps as
a religious project for an individual it is as good as
any, but the political attempt to implement it in a
society composed of people most of whom do not
even aspire to sainthood, much less come within
spitting distance (as we say) of attaining it, can lead
only to repression.

Adopting Dewey's idea, I can see myself as living
in a variety of overlapping publics. When someone
in my street is playing the radio too loudly, the relevant "other" members of the public are those

within earshot, and we may "take care of" those consequences by making an agreement with one another to regulate the use of radios, an agreement enforced by informal social pressure. If I were to come into the university to lecture one day drunk, this might enhance my performance sufficiently to move the "public," that is, the students in the audience, to set up a fund and delegate one of their number to meet with me in a bar before every lecture, so as to ensure that I am always adequately prepared. If there is a proposal before the City Council to reduce congestion and air pollution in town by closing certain streets to passage by motor vehicles and providing for more cycle paths, the relevant "public" is everyone who might ride a bicycle, everyone who might be affected, positively or negatively, by the changed traffic flow, and everyone who pays the taxes from which the cycle paths will be funded. Associated with the different publics are different public goods (and evils) and different possible ways of "taking care of" or regulating consequences. Obviously public goods (relative to the same or different publics) might conflict: providing more cycle paths might make it more difficult for some elderly or infirm pedestrians to cross a certain street.

Not every public has a common or public good. Three persons struggling to stay afloat on a plank

that will only bear the weight of one have no common good or, at any rate, no practically feasible
common good, although, of course, one can say
that it would be better for all concerned if the situation as a whole were different from what it is, and
one could fantasize about what their common
good would be if they were not in the situation
they are in, but in a different one, say, one in which
they were struggling to get into a lifeboat that
could easily accommodate three. None of these re-
flections on different hypothetical situations, however, is a thought about what is a common good
for them in their real situation. Perhaps they do not
constitute a "public" in Dewey's sense, because
there are no "systematic" consequences to be cared
for—after this one-off encounter, two of them, at
least, will be dead. Still we can easily imagine orga-
nized societies existing in circumstances of extreme deprivation, in which there simply was no
policy that would be good for the society as a
whole or "the people." Whatever anyone does,
some will live and many will die. If there is no public good, then, *a fortiori*, there cannot be a nonde-
ceptive shared public conception of the (public)
good in such a society.

One might wonder whether in addition to all
the particular "publics" of which we are members—cyclists, gardeners, self-defeatingly abstemi-

ous university lecturers, taxpayers, lovers of si-
lence—there was some single world public of all
humans or even of all sentient or rational beings.
Whether or not there is such a public, it seems
unlikely that there is any public good associated
with it. I do not mean to ask whether the good of
humanity as a whole should take precedence over
the good of cyclists but rather whether there even
is any such thing as the good of humanity as a
whole. Some people, particularly liberals, seem to
think it quite obvious that there must be. The re-
ceived liberal view generally assumes that one
must take people as they come and never treat
them in a paternalist way, that for any group of
such people there will be a rational common good
to which they all, *in principle*, have access and
which they can come to know by free discussion.
To be sure, to realize fully the public good may
require some changes in existing practices, but
these will be of the nature of reforms.

This approach, with its emphasis on consensus,
nonviolence, and discussion, seems very humane,
and it can work quite well in the everyday politics
of relatively affluent societies with stable institutions and a homogeneous liberal consensus on
basic values and assumptions; however, such societies constitute only a small portion of the political

world in which we live.[21] An alternative to this whole approach to politics, and one I myself find much more plausible, is offered by Georg Lukács in *Geschichte und Klassenbewußtsein*. Lukács thought about the question of what it would mean for a society as a whole to be a single "self-conscious subject" (as he called it).[22] One thing we could say for sure, he thought, was that there could be no such self-conscious subject in a society that was split into antagonistic classes with radically incompatible interests. There is no single common good in a society in which whatever is good for the proletariat is bad for capitalists and vice versa, and any form of consciousness that pretended to embody such a common neutral good could be nothing other than ideological delusion. Only in a society without private ownership of means of production, and thus without classes, would it even be possible to see society as a whole coherently from a single point of view. Only in a classless society, that is, could there be any such thing as a common or public good, or a shared public conception of the good that was not based on gross illusions. Under current circumstances, Lukács thought, politics as usual was a pointless activity, a matter of slaves quarreling among themselves over inadequate rations or slaveholders engaged in empty struggles for prestige and precedence. The remedy was class warfare on the part of the proletariat under the leadership of a vanguard party that would change the rules of the game and bring into existence a form of society in which a unitary "public good" was possible. In various ways, Lukács's position now looks antiquated. He seems to make a number of assumptions about the unity of the human subject that seem implausible—if no individual has a single unitary self-consciousness but we are all more or less gerry-rigged, multilayered collections of psychic systems moved by obscure and irreducibly contradictory impulses, why then should one expect any society to be self-transparent in its pursuit of completely unitary goals? This may be true, but it does nothing to rehabilitate the notion that there will be a universal public good; in fact, if anything, it makes it seem even less plausible that it could exist. If the scenario that describes the inevitable confrontation of proletariat and capitalist classes as representatives of the single overarching contradiction that constitutes modern societies also seems passé, that does not necessarily mean that we now know that social harmony and rational consensus reign, or even potentially could reign, throughout the world. The real world, on the contrary, is criss-crossed with divisions and swarming with tribes, corporations, states, social movements, alliances, "nations," oppressing and oppressed populations who have radically different resources, power, institutional structures and conceptions of the good. Instead of Lukács' assumption of "one major contradiction," that between labor and capital, we have innumerable, entrenched antagonistic groups with sometimes highly articulated and deeply incompatible interests. Finally, Lukács' own solution seems naive because we have reason to believe that there are many more entrenched differences in power and sources of irreconcilable conflict than he countenanced. Surely that gives us no reason to be optimistic about the possible existence of a state of social harmony and consensus, or the existence of a universal public good.

It may *sometimes* happen that in a real or a hypothetical discussion (under imagined ideal circumstances) one can (or could) find commonality, points on which one can agree, neutral ground to which one can retreat, or a common, public good, but I see no reason to believe that this will invariably or even usually be the case. The possibilities of real or hypothetical agreement and consensus in the world are extremely limited. This does not, of course, imply that it might not be an extremely good idea to conduct as extensive discussions as possible, develop discursive institutions, and so on. We might have all kinds of good reasons for this apart from the excessively cheerful idea that free discussion would give us automatic access to a common good. It certainly does not seem unreasonable to prefer discussion to violence, especially if one lives in affluence and is confronted with armed have-nots.

One can, of course, *say* and imagine various things about a purported "common" or "public" good, for instance, that "the public good" (of the whole world population) would require equalization of resources between those persons and groups who are currently rich and those who are currently poor, the haves and the have-nots, and also draconian measures to reduce population, stop depletion of natural resources, and reverse the pollution of the environment. This is a bit like saying of the three people clinging to the plank that the public good would require that they be in a lifeboat or that each of them have a flotation vest; true enough, and if each was a fish, they could all swim happily away. To make this claim, however, in abstraction from an account of the actual political and economic circumstances, the possible mechanisms of action, and the probable results of adopting any concrete available course of action is perhaps an interesting speculation, and all human beings are understandably fascinated with such

productions of the imagination, but it is not an ac-
tion-orienting proposal of any kind. What will *really* happen in the world depends on the actual
causal constitution of the world. One thing we
know about the political and social world is that it
is a large, unsurveyable, and extremely unwieldy
object that seems sometimes to be hopelessly inert
and at others suprisingly mercurial. We also know
that it is composed of highly disparate parts that
seem to operate very differently from one another,
almost to stand under different laws. Finally, we
know only too well that we are grossly ignorant of
how these laws actually operate and what mechanisms could be employed effectively to bring about
particular desired results. It would be a mistake to
think that "the problem" is that most of the relevant actors are corrupt governments, bloodthirsty
and overexcited bodies of armed men, predatory
financial and commercial enterprises, and weak,
ill-informed, and misguided international organi-
zations. There are, of course, enough corrupt governments to go around, but Hobbes allows us to
see that the central problem is not moral failing
but the mere existence of an unstructured world
with separate, epistemically mutually opaque centers of independent power and initiative, pursuing
courses of action that are not unreasonable given

the circumstances. Hobbes himself thought there were "laws of nature," general principles found out by reason, by appeal to which we could mitigate the inconveniences of our state.[23] To arrive at a realistic assessment of the modern predicament, one must, however, add to Hobbes's view a Nietzschean skepticism about "reason."[24] The actual transfer of the assets of the one thousand greediest and most successful international corporations to *any* single existing agency or set of agencies (the UN, the WHO, the Taliban, NATO, etc.), abstracting from the issue of how politically one could even do this, would probably not in fact be liable to bring the purported universal "public good" into existence. The have-nots may not fail to point out how convenient this conclusion is to the haves (and to the intellectual classes that are their mouthpiece). From the fact that it is convenient it does not necessarily follow that it is not also true. No other obviously feasible political action would work either. Marx used the term *utopian* to designate imaginary conceptions of the good proposed without any connection to possible political means of realizing them; this is an extremely charitable way to describe them. Finally, for there to be a feasible common good for the world might require that some of us, some individuals and some types of individuals, say the 600 million or so over-privileged consumers of the developed world, sim-ply did not exist. To bring this about would be not "reform" but "revolution," a transformation in which, in a relatively short time, whole classes and types of people simply go out or, more usually, are put out of existence. This, of course, too, is a fan-tasy. In the postrevolutionary situation there might, perhaps, be *a* common public good, but it would not be *our* common public good because we would not exist. In the long run that is bound to happen, because individual human beings all die eventually and social types change, but in the short run it is unlikely, and if it does happen soon on a large scale it will probably be as a result of accidental catastro-phe or of comprehensible but wild forms of large-scale social vengeance, not of political decision or social planning. The consequences of such an even-tuality are now, in any case, inestimable.

Despite the attractiveness of some of the values liberals have defended, in some respects the liberal approach is not just a mistake but is itself part of the problem, at least to the extent that it is com-mitted, in its contemporary form, to indefeasible private property rights as the core of a "private sphere." Perhaps the same is true of the liberal po-litical principle that one should take people as they are, nonpaternalistically, allowing them to be the best judges of what is good for them and recognizing no good apart from what is good for particular individuals. For the foreseeable future, in any case, we will be stuck with a welter of various kinds of goods, some private, some public, with no clear principle for structuring them under a single conception of a unitary public good.

CONCLUSION

The purported "right to privacy" is unusual in that one can document the exact moment it was first formulated. It was invented in a paper written by Samuel Warren and Louis Brandeis in 1890.[1] Warren's wife, a rich society lady, deeply disapproved that newspapers were publishing reports about the parties she gave, and her husband set about concocting a reason for imposing restrictions on such reporting. Judith Jarvis Thomson has argued very persuasively[2] that this right does not exist in the sense that it fails to designate any kind of coherent single property or single interest. That does not mean that none of the various things that have come to be grouped under "privacy" are goods—far from it, many of them are extremely important and valuable—only that they are disparate goods, and the perfectly adequate grounds we have for trying to promote them have little to do with one another. My general suggestion is that what Thomson argues for the purported "right to

privacy" holds in spades for the more general category of "the private" as contrasted with "the public." There is no such thing as *the* public/private
distinction, or, at any rate, it is a deep mistake to
think that there is a single substantive distinction
here that can be made to do any real philosophical
or political work. When one begins to look at it
carefully, the purported distinction between public
and private begins to dissolve into a number of issues that have relatively little to do with one another. It is thus unlikely one could come up with
an interesting, general, substantive theory of the
public and private. This does not *in itself* mean that
any particular thing—object, institution, feature of
human life, and so on—that is now valued as a special public or private good is unimportant or not
really valuable. It does suggest, however, that it
would be a good idea for us to think again before
appealing unreflectively to "the public/private distinction" in justificatory contexts.

To repeat this as a methodological point: it is
not the case that we must or should adopt a two-
step procedure, *first* getting clear about the public/
private distinction, assuming all the while that
there is a single distinction to be made, and *then*,
having discovered where the line falls between
public and private, going on to ask what we can do
with that distinction, what attitude we should

adopt toward it, what implications making the distinction correctly might have for politics. Rather, *first* we must ask what this purported distinction is *for*, that is, *why* we want to make it at all. To answer this question will bring us back to some relatively concrete context of human action, probably human political action, and it is only in the context of connecting the issue of the public and private to that antecedent potential context of political action that the distinction will make any sense. It is thus a mistake to answer the question, "Why shouldn't we interfere with that?" with "*Because* it is private," and think that this is the obvious end of the discussion. In itself it merely and tautologically says that we should not interfere because that is the kind of thing we think we ought not to interfere with. By saying it is private, we just shift the locus of the argument to the question of *why* we think we ought not to interfere, and the reasons we give for this will be highly diverse; that is, in modern societies the cash value of the claim "This is private" is usually that noted by Dewey: "We think this sphere of activity is of sufficient interest and importance to you, and its effects on others are of sufficiently little importance, for us to think we ought to refrain in interfering in it or regulating it." The question this raises is, of course, "of sufficient importance" in *whose* judgment: that of

the "you" whose action will or will not be interfered with, that of the "others" on which the action
will or will not have an effect, or that of some
third-party authorities who are responsible for de-
ciding how much regulation, and regulation of
what sort, the society will organize?

We have no great difficulty now in classifying as
"private" the goods Diogenes and Augustine pur-
sued, an *askesis*-based self-sufficiency in the case of
Diogenes and spirituality in the case of Augustine,
or in classifying the *Pax Romana* as "public," although many people did not think the *Pax* a
"good"[3] and although the establishment and maintenance of the *Pax* involved large numbers of people ruthlessly pursuing various private interests.
With Socrates the situation becomes a bit more
complex because we see him through the eyes of
Plato, who has an interest in presenting his project
as both—indeed at the same time—care of the self
(a kind of private good) and improvement of the
citizens of the city (surely a public good). Discom-
fort arises not only because Socrates wrote nothing
and so we are dependent on Plato's opinion of
what Socrates' quest amounted to rather than
more direct sources, but also because we do not
believe that psychological/moral/private and polit-
ical/public can fit together quite as comfortably as
Plato would have us believe.[4] The correct conclu-

sion to draw from this is not, I think, the one Rorty suggests,[5] namely, that we should hold fast to the public/private distinction and accept that the two sides need to be kept strictly separate.[6] Why *always* police a quarantine line between the routine, responsible prose of legislation and collective action, on the one hand, and vivid metaphors of human aspiration, on the other? We do not have a clear grasp, not even a rough-and-ready nontheoretical grasp, of the two categories of public and private as marking out two clearly distinct domains. Rather, each of these categories is a disordered jumble of different things; the distinction between public and private is not neat (Rorty), but neither are the two ideally, or even non-ideally, coordinate and conformable to each other (Plato). To repeat, there is no single distinction between public and private; the various senses of "public" do not cohere very closely with one another, nor do the senses of "private"; the various forms of opposition between "public" and "private" are neither absolute nor are they all, in the final instance, insubstantial and illusory. This does not mean we should simply leave the whole issue unexamined and not even worry about how the various items are related to one another. We can and should ask whether the private ideal of spirituality is something for which we want to make a public place in our society. That my neighbors are all fantasizing about the violent righting of historical or metaphysical wrongs is not just a fact about a collection of private self-images but also a social fact that can be seen to have a public dimension even if our mode of access to it is highly indirect and fallible.[7] Fantasies are not "real" acts, but they are also not unconnected with real acts. Even if there is some austere epistemic privacy to individual reflection, as a general practice it will have an aspect that is visible to others, and may have an effect on them.

Some distinctions we make in everyday life do seem to be rooted in features of the human condition and to have basic standing in thinking about politics. By saying that they have "basic standing," I do not mean that they have any peculiar or special metaphysical status or that a proper understanding of them will, by itself, tell us automatically how to structure our political life, only that they are factors on which we will have to fix our attention carefully and have reflective views, if we want to be serious about understanding politics. Thus Hobbes observed that humans are finite, dangerous to one another, biologically motivated to seek self-preservation, and ignorant of one another's intentions and beliefs. That I do not immediately know what beliefs and values a stranger whom I encounter has, and also do not immediately know what his or her intentions are toward me, *is* a basic fact about human life as we know it, and one fully compatible with Wittgenstein's criticisms of essentialism and of philosophical notions of "privacy." It may not be the case that rational reflection on these observations, particularly on the centrality to humans of the drive to self-preservation in conditions of uncertainty, leads to the conclusion that Hobbes prefers. Others, certainly, have put a very different construction on these facts. Hegel, for example, claimed that it is essential to humans to be able to overcome their biological urge to self-preservation and to risk their lives for the sake of some conception of themselves as entities of a certain kind (self-defining origins of desire).[8] Some philosophers, for instance Nietzsche, have gone even further down this road, claiming not merely that the urge to self-assertion or to the assertion of a relatively abstract "identity" is a necessary part of what it is to be human, but that in some sense, at least in the case of the most admirable type of human, it should take systematic priority over the routine structures of self-preservation.[9] Hegel had no difficulty admitting both a desire for self-preservation and a desire for self-assertion because he thought that, although these two urges might in their more extreme forms point in opposite directions, it was still possible to create political and social structures that rendered the two drives compatible. These were structures based on the "mutual recognition" of human agents. In processes of "recognition," Hegel claimed, a place was found for a form of self-assertion that was not socially destructive.[10] The question is whether this view of the nature of Western political and social institutions and of the possibility of taming self-assertion without stunting human vitality is not wildly optimistic. Nietzsche thought it was.[11]

However, even this Hegelian demurral from Hobbes does not ignore or fail to recognize the facts Hobbes cites. Hegel agrees that the features of the human situation Hobbes cites are ones on which one must have a considered opinion. The public/private distinction, I am claiming, does not have the fundamental status of human finitude, mutual ignorance, or the urges for self-preservation and self-assertion. Furthermore, none of these leads in any obvious way to liberal doctrines like antipaternalism, limitation of state powers, and so on. To the extent to which there *is* a component of the public/private distinction that seems to have special human centrality, it is precisely the Hobbesian point about "public" mutual ignorance of the "private" intentions of individuals in the state of nature. Hobbes combines this with a view that would seem grist to liberalism's mill—that "good" and "evil" do not exist "in the nature of the objects themselves" but only in relation to the person who uses these terms[12]—and uses the conjunction to argue for the necessity of an authoritarian absolute state.

So I wish to suggest that to make a *practically significant* distinction between public and private, a distinction, that is, that deserves to have moral, existential, social, or political standing, we first need a clear idea of the use to which we wish to put the distinction when we have made it. The first question is this: *Why* exactly do we want to distinguish private and public? What are our purposes and values? Because we can have a variety of different (legitimate) purposes, we can have a legitimate plurality of different ways of distinguishing between the two. From the fact that we do not begin with an ontologically realist account of the distinction[13] *as a single, unitary distinction*, it does not follow that we cannot come to a rationally well-supported view that gives us reason to distinguish them for particular purposes in particular contexts. It follows only that the "reason" we will use will be a contextually located human power, not some abstract faculty of reading off the moral demands of the universe from the facts of the case. To put the same thing another way, it is not as if there were simply *nothing* for our concepts and theories to track in the case of "the private" and "the public," in the sense that there is nothing for zoological theories of unicorns to track.[14] Rather, there are many *different* things to track, but tracking them distinctly requires knowing why you might want to catch them, and failure to distinguish will lead into a dismal conceptual swamp from which it will be very difficult to extricate oneself unmuddied.

Much as we might regret it, we are in fact living in a time and at a place in which we do not really have any effective general framework for thinking about politics apart from liberalism,[15] so the main place that a distinction between public and private occupies in such a general scheme is in the context of a defense of the "private sphere" from encroachment by the public, where that public is construed as the coercive apparatus of government, the heavy, pervasive hortatory blandishment of administrative agencies, or the subtle pressure of public opinion. It may be useful, though, to remind ourselves that this is the highly parochial problem of a particular kind of society that has thrown itself with a will into a certain very specific process of economic and political development while being unable either fully to embrace or fully to free itself from certain remnants of the Christian worldview.

NOTES

Chapter I. Introduction

1. The most convenient modern edition of this is in M. Gauchet, ed., *De la liberté chez les modernes: Écrits politiques*.

2. Constant, *De la liberté chez les modernes*, pp. 184 ff.

3. Ibid., p. 495

4. Ibid., p. 183

5. See, e.g., C. Nicolet, *Le métier de citoyen dans la Rome republicaine*.

6. Constant, *De la liberté chez les modernes*, p. 184

7. von Humboldt, *Ideen zu einem Versuch*, vol. 1, pp. 56–234.

8. Mill, *On Liberty*, esp. chap. 4.

9. This group will include Max Weber, Isaiah Berlin, Hayek, Habermas, Richard Rorty, Michael Walzer, and any contemporary theorist or political actor who has been seriously influenced by Mill's *On Liberty*.

10. Cf. Bok, *Secrets: On the Ethics of Concealment and Revelation*.

11. Cf. Hölscher, *Öffentlichkeit und Geheimnis*. I take it, at any rate, that this is the contemporary meaning. In the past, of course, *arcanum* could mean something that was the privileged information or knowledge of a restricted group, as in "*arcana imperii*."

Chapter II. Shamelessness and the Public World

1. Major source is Diogenes Laertius 6. §§ 20–81. See also Dudley, *A History of Cynicism*; and Niehues-Pröbsting, *Der*

115

Kynismus des Diogenes und der Begriff des Kynismus. Questions have been raised about the veracity of the reports we have about Diogenes. Important as it is to get the facts right, to the extent to which that is possible, my intention in this essay is not, in the first instance, historical, so I will ignore the many interesting issues that arise about the reliability of the various sources. The same thing holds for the story of Krates and Hipparchia, and the claim about what Caesar said before crossing the Rubicon (both treated later in this book).

2. Elias, *Über den Prozeß der Zivilisation.* This work has been extensively criticized in Duerr's *Der Mythos vom Zivilisationsprozeß*, which is announced as comprising four volumes: *Nacktheit und Scham* (1988), *Intimität* (1990), *Obszönität und Gewalt* (1993); I have not yet seen the promised fourth volume.

3. Diogenes Laertius 6. § 46.

4. Cf. Goffman, *Behavior in Public Places*; *Stigmas*; *Presentation of Self in Everyday Life*; and *Frame Analysis*. Epicurus' slogan, "λάθε βιώσας" ("live unnoticed"), might seem to be a variant of this idea of "civil inattention." It is usually interpreted, however, as advice to withdraw from the political world into the world of "private life," not as a guide on how to behave in public.

5. Goffman describes this phenomenon and calls it "stigmatization" (see his *Stigmas*).

6. The distinction I have in mind between (4) and (5) is the following: I can fail to exercise a competence I have, for instance, the ability to greet you appropriately when you come up to me, because I am concentrating on some task I have at hand, and think the accomplishing of that task is more important than politeness. In doing this I perform a voluntary act of failing to greet you, but I don't *intend* to insult you. Insulting you—if that is what happens—is a mere

by-product of my action, one that I take no steps to prevent but that is not part of my intention. Thus I might be very pleased if you were not insulted by my behavior here. This case, an instance of (4), is distinct from the case in which what I set out to do is willfully to insult you by failing to greet you.

7. Diogenes Laertius 6. § 58.

8. The tense relation in which this principle stands to the phenomena of "conspicuous consumption" (and its potential role in legitimizing forms of political and social authority) would repay discussion. For an extremely stimulating discussion of ancient "euergetism," cf. Veyne, *Le pain et le cirque*.

9. This second principle might seem to be just a subcase of the first. If the society is one in which near starvation is not unusual, anyone eating in public *will ipso facto* be violating the principle of disattendability, because the more likely it is that others who are starving will be present, the more diffi- cult it will be to ignore them. Since the question of whether there is one principle here or two does not seem to me terri- bly important, I will not discuss this further.

10. Diogenes Laertius 6. § 27.

11. See Miller, *The Anatomy of Disgust*, and Menninghaus, *Ekel*. For further classic discussions of "disgust," cf. Kant *Kritik der Urteilskraft*, § 48; Rosenkranz *Die Ästhetik des Häß- lichen*; Nietzsche *Die Geburt der Tragödie* § 7; *Jenseits von Gut und Böse* § 26; *Zur Genealogie der Moral* 3. 13–26; and Kri- steva, *Pouvoirs de l'horreur*. The work of Kolnai on this topic, "*Der Ekel*," is of particular importance as a remarkably clear and wide-ranging account. One influential account of "pollu- tion" is Douglas, *Purity and Danger*.

12. For the sake of simplicity of exposition I will speak interchangeably in what follows of "polluted," "dirty/filthy," or "foul." Actually, of course, there are nuances of difference

in the way these terms are used. "Polluted" refers in the first instance to things or states of affairs that fail to satisfy various religious, transcendental, or ritual standards (especially if there is considered to be a possibility of contagion, the transfer of such pollution by contact or association). "Dirty/filthy" refers to a more secular category of "matter out of place." "Foul" seems to refer more specifically to a state of organic decay. For people who take the category of "pollution" seriously, for example, those who take certain traditional religious views seriously, a ritually "pure" meal or dish can be (secularly) "dirty/ filthy" (covered with dust, flies, etc.).

13. See the discussion of Augustine chapter 4, below.

14. Of course, other things having no direct connection with human bodily functions can also be considered dirty, be objects of disgust, and so on.

15. Kolnai rightly emphasizes the close connection of feelings of disgust with reactions to that which is or seems to be either excessively full of life—teeming swarms of insects—or recently deprived of life—corpses, rotten meat. Dead things that look alive or living things that look moribund are preeminent objects of disgust. This might well be connected with our sense that disgust is often aroused by dissolution of boundaries, loss of firm outline and definition, mixtures of various kinds, and so on. The basic reaction of disgust would then be a reaction to what reminds us of death, and what "really" reminds us of death are not nonorganic states or even fully dead objects but things that look as if they were about to go over from life to death, for example, meat full of swarming maggots. Our experience of disgust results from our own "metaphysical nearness" to death: "unser Bestehen aus todgeweihter, man könnte sagen, todestrunkener, verwesungsbereiter Materie" (pp. 558 f). ("The fact that we consist of matter that is doomed to die, that, one could say, is drunk

with death and ripe for decay" [trans. RG]). Menninghaus, however, points out that excessive sweetness can also cause disgust and suggests that certain post-romantic aesthetic phenomena can be seen to be connected with a desire to avoid a disgust that would arise from satiation with the beautiful (*Ekel*, pp. 40–50).

16. Note, however, Kolnai's exceedingly astute set of distinctions between the phenomenology of angst and that of disgust.

17. Freud, *Das Unbehagen in der Kultur*, p. 229 f. (footnote). The "teaching" can, of course, take a more or less repressive form. Even if Freud is right (*Drei Abhandlungen zur Sexualtheorie*, pp. 84–86) that the construction of a sense of disgust as a "dam" against the satisfaction of deviant sexual desires is "organically conditioned" (*organisch bedingt*) and merely helped along by training (*Erziehung*)—and how exactly would Freud *know* that?—the form the *Erziehung* takes in a certain society may be covertly (or overtly) violent. In any case, one may assume that there would be a tendency to overlook or downplay whatever amount of coercion was required because of the difficulty we have imagining a settled human social life in which the learning in question did not take place.

18. I am now making a further simplifying assumption. In the rest of the main text I will speak as if there is a one-to-one connection between increasing filthiness/pollution on the part of the object and increasing disgust on the part of the subject. Unfortunately things are not as straightforward as that. I need not be disgusted by filth/dirt or by the polluted. On the other hand, I may have a reaction of disgust to things that cannot reasonably be considered "polluted" or "dirty/filthy" (e.g., the skin that forms on the top of hot milk when it cools; cf. Kristeva, *Pouvoirs de l'horreur*, p. 10). Cf.

Mill, *On Liberty*, p. 85. Needless to say, reactions of disgust are qualitatively completely different from *simple* distaste, for example, not "caring for" the taste of coffee.

19. Shame, of course, is in some ways a wider and in some ways a narrower phenomenon than disgust. I ought to be ashamed to be seen doing something disgusting, but I can also feel shame at exhibiting a weakness or incompetence or a vice that is in no way disgusting. On the other hand, I can be disgusting without being shameless; I may simply fail to have the usual control over some of my bodily functions, do all I can to mitigate the results, but still feel ashamed at my failure to be able to exercise successful control. One would need, then, a minimum of five categories: (1) what causes fear/angst versus what does not, (2) dirt/filthy versus clean, (3) polluted versus pure, (4) disgusting versus not disgusting, and (6) shameful versus not shameful. I cannot explore further here the question of how "shame/shameful" relates to the other four. For further discussion of "shame," cf. Dodds, *The Greeks and the Irrational*; and Williams, *Shame and Necessity*.

20. To act as if a relation of intimacy existed can, of course, be itself an insulting presumption; cf. Geuss, *Parrots, Poets, Philosophers, and Good Advice*, pp. 32–33 (Martial 10.15).

21. See Miller, *The Anatomy of Disgust*, chap. 6.

22. Of course, liberalism does not just comprise a doctrine of the toleration of divergent opinions but also of divergent ways of living. See also chapter 5, below.

23. For Cynic notions of *askesis*, cf. Goulet-Cazé, *Ascèse Cynique*. The emperor Julian also emphasizes how easy it is to become a Cynic (*Oratio 6*).

24. Oddly enough, the Cynics had a theory of training to inure themselves to natural hardship but did not have a similar form of exercise for learning to ignore cultural norms.

They seemed to think such a thing unnecessary. You had to *learn* and *train* yourself to sleep in the cold without a roof, but you did not need to learn to masturbate and defecate in public, to eat human flesh, and so on. These later came "naturally" when you once saw that there was no ὀρθὸς λόγος against them. Unfortunately this seems not to be true. At any rate, once one has had a certain upbringing that will include learning to experience disgust at certain things, that reaction will not disappear naturally once one sees that it is based on a false belief. That this whole area of phenomena has this property of straddling the culture/nature is unfortunate for the Cynics, because they need a strict distinction here. Their theory depends on being able to distinguish these two things and focus on that which is natural while rejecting the conventional. Nietzsche is especially good on the uselessness of the distinction between nature and culture. See his *Jenseits von Gut und Böse*, §§ 9, 188.

25. Cf. Wilamowitz-Moellendorff's introduction to his edition of Euripides' *Herakles*, vol. 1, pp. 1–170, for a good general treatment of the figure of Herakles in early literature.

26. Cf. Aristophanes *Birds* 1583 ff.; and Euripides *Alcestis* 747–802.

27. Diogenes Laertius 6. § 63.

28. Augustine notes this in the remark I cite below (chap. 4) from *City of God* (14.20).

29. In Plato's *Apology* (19b) Socrates says that one of the things he is accused of is being a busybody: "Σωκράτης ἀδικεῖ καὶ περιεργάζεται."

30. "βδελυρός" by Thrasymachos in *Republic* (338d). The word seems to come from the onomatopoetic word for "to break wind" (βδέω). One of Theophrastus' "characters" is the "βδελυρός," the "stinker." See also Geuss, *Parrots, Poets, Philosophers, and Good Advice*, pp. 20–21.

31. *Apology* 23b.
32. *Apology* 31c–32e.
33. *Phaedrus* 230b–e.
34. *Crito* 52a–c.
35. *Apology* 36c–d.
36. *Gorgias* 521d.
37. Diogenes Laertius 6.54.

CHAPTER III. *RES PUBLICA*

1. My account of this is obviously dependent on Christian Meier; *see* his "Caesars Bürgerkrieg," in his *Entstehung des Begriffs "Demokratie,"* pp. 70–150; also see his *Caesar*.

2. Although in many contexts the Romans contrasted *publicus* with *priuatus*, they sometimes used a tripartite distinction between *publicus, priuatus,* and *sacer* as in their distinction between three kinds of laws: (a) "public," concerning magistracies; (b) "private," concerning relations between individuals, especially property relations; and (c) "sacred" concerning the gods and their cult.

3. I am particularly indebted to Peter Garnsey for comments on the first version of this chapter.

4. Following Lucian Hölscher, *Öffentlichkeit und Geheimnis,* esp. pp. 40–43. Hölscher extends his analysis in his entry *"öffentlich"* (*s.v.*) in Brunner, Conze, and Kosellek, *Geschichtliche Grundbegriffe.* For a further, more extensive discussion of this point along the same lines, cf. Nicolet, *Le métier de citoyen dans la Rome republicaine,* chap. 3 ("Militia"). For a discussion of some parallel phenomena in early medieval Europe, see D. Green, *Language and History in the Early Germanic World* (Cambridge University Press, 1998), esp. chap. 5.

5. Traces of this attitude remained in place even in the second half of the twentieth century. Thus, even as late as the 1970s, young men subject to conscription in France could be prosecuted for attempting to commit suicide on the grounds that they were trying to damage essential military equipment. Zeev Emmerich informs me that Israel has, or until very recently had, similar legislation. Peter Brown describes this ancient view in contrasting it with the Christian attitude that was to succeed it: "Christian attitudes to sexuality delivered a deathblow to the ancient notion of the city as arbiter of the body. . . . [The body] was no longer a neutral, indeterminate outcrop of the natural world, whose use and very right to exist was subject to predominantly civic considerations of status and utility" (*The Body and Society*, p. 437).

6. There is an instructive parallel here with Max Weber's view of the importance of democracy to a modern state; see, especially, his "Wahlrecht und Demokratie in Deutschland" (originally published in 1917; now in *Gesammelte politische Schriften*). Those in the tradition descending from Rousseau emphasize the inherent merits of a democratic form of government. It is good in itself that the people rule itself. Weber, on the contrary, seems to hold that, in the modern world, democracy is the unavoidable political form because only a democratic state can muster enough internal consensus to be an effective international actor.

7. Cf. passages cited above, in notes 1–4 of chapter 1.

8. Cf. Marx, *Grundrisse*, p. 387.

9. Herodotos 7.144.

10. This allowed the Athenians to indict persons making proposals that were *retrospectively* deemed illegal, even if those proposals had originally been carried in the Assembly. *Cf. Der kleine Pauly* (s.v.).

11. This means that claims like those found in Wirszub-ski, *Libertas as a Political Ideal at Rome*, p. 3 ("The Roman State recognized and protected the freedom of those foreign-ers alone who were citizens of States which concluded a treaty with Rome," are entirely misleading. If the line of argument I expound in the main text is correct, the entry in the *Oxford Latin Dictionary* that gives "the State" as one meaning of *res publica* (cf. *s.v.*, is also wrong. Cf. Suerbaum, *Vom antiken zum frühmittelalterlichen Staatsbegriff*; and Drexler, *Politische Grundbegriffe der Römer*; cf. also the various older German works cited in Hölscher, *Öffentlichkeit und Geheimnis*; and Skinner, "The State." Characteristically, one of the earliest systematic thinkers who does have a rather clear conception of the "state," Hobbes, uses it as the equivalent of the Latin term *ciuitas*, not of *res publica* (cf., e.g., *Leviathan*, p. 9).

12. The main difficulty in thinking about the relation of "public" and "private" in Rome, or, for that matter, in think-ing about the concept of *res publica*, is to recognize that the Romans did have a distinction between *publicus* and *priuatus* but did *not* have a concept of the "state." For us, it is ex-tremely difficult to imagine a social formation in which there is an existing status quo of distribution of power for dealing with matters of common concern, and yet this is not located in a sociologically separate structure.

13. From the fact that magistrates had authority over (some) matters of concern to everyone, it neither followed that they had unlimited or undivided authority nor that they had authority outside a relatively small area of competence. Bridges are of common concern to all, but to have a public responsibility for bridges does not imply having any kind of authority over weights and measures in the marketplace.

14. I believe that a distinction is also sometimes made be-tween the "*potentia*" or "*potestas*" of the assemblies of the peo-

ple and the "*auctoritas*" of the Senate. This might be thought to conform roughly to a distinction between having the effective power to do something and having the normative warrant that arises from following the good advice of those who have had wide experience.

15. For the sake of simplicity of exposition I will speak of an "individual" who is not a magistrate, but the same account would hold for a subgroup of the army that was not composed of magistrates. Such a subgroup could hold property, have concerns, and a collective good; these would all be "*res priuatae*."

16. Kantorowicz shows, in *The King's Two Bodies*, how difficult it was for medievals to formulate this distinction.

17. Thus, in the absence of a system of regular salaries, Roman magistrates who were sent out to administer provinces, especially during the late Republican period, were tacitly allowed, as it were, to live off the land, as long as this remained within reasonable limits. It was not always clear, however, what those limits were, and even when it was it was difficult to enforce them. Max Weber is especially good on the role of a trained administrative staff—a group of professional bureaucrats with an appropriate technical apparatus— in the modern state. See his *Politik als Beruf* in *Gesammelte politische Schriften*, pp. 508–13.

18. Appian *Civil War* 2 § 35: "ἡ μὲν ἐπίσχεσις, ὦ φίλοι, τῆσδε τῆς διαβάσεως ἐμοὶ κακῶν ἄρξει, ἡ δὲ διάβασις πᾶσιν ἀνθρώποις" (literally, "Refraining from this crossing will be the start of evils for me, my friends, but the crossing will be the start of evils for all humans").

19. The Latin expressions from which our word *interest* is derived were used in context of *disagreement* and seem originally to have had a strong connotation of the particularity of the "interest" being ascribed, that is, an "interest" was

precisely *not* something that was shared or common but something of differential concern to a particular person, *as opposed to* other persons. Thus the original distinction would have been between "common good" and "individual interest." Only later does the notion of a potentially shared or common or "public" interest become established. For reasons of space, I have not made any attempt in this book to observe various more subtle distinctions that would actually have to be made here, and so I speak more or less interchangeably of "common good," "common interest," "public interest," and so on.

20. Thus one of the ways that tyranny eventually came to be distinguished from more legitimate forms of government was that the tyrant ruled in his own interest. Cf. Aristotle *Politics* Book 3.

21. The standard older work on *raison d'état* is Meinecke's *Die Idee der Staatsräson*.

Chapter IV. The Spiritual and the Private

1. *De civ. Dei* 14.20. He is presumably referring to the so-called κυνογάμια, the "dogs' marriage," of Krates and Hipparchia. Hipparchia of Maroneia, the only woman to whom a separate entry in Diogenes Laertius' *Lives and Opinions of the Great Philosophers* is devoted, fell in love with the Cynic philosopher Krates, and he insisted she adopt his mode of life as a condition of marrying her.

2. See Brown, *Augustine of Hippo*, chapter 11.

3. *Confessiones* 10. 8.

4. It has often been noted that metaphors of the eye dominate much of Greek thought, so that what was considered to

be most important was correctly recognizing the visual aspect or appearance of things (*ideai*). Christianity follows Ju-
daism in giving a kind of priority to metaphors derived from
the ear: The Jewish God has no visible form, and what is
most important is hearing, acknowledging, and obeying the
injunctions issuing from an overwhelmingly powerful, external, invisible source. For a discussion about visual as opposed
to other forms of representation of God, cf. Halbertal and
Margalit, *Idolatry*. Since *reflection* is a term deriving from the
sphere of vision, one might feel some hesitation about using
it for a self-referential conversation like a confession. Memory is not a repository of geometric figures surveyable at a
glance (a panopticon) for Augustine but a series of courts and
halls through which one must wander. It is, then, perhaps
significant that the crucial moment of Augustine's conversion comes when he hears the voice of an invisible child re-
peating an imperative: "tolle lege tolle lege" ("Pick up and
read; pick up and read") (*Confessiones* 8.12). Plato's *Republic*,
on the contrary, begins with Socrates wanting to watch a fes-
tival (βουλόμενος θεάσασθαι 327a).

5. Thus confession to God is like psychoanalysis in that
the psychoanalyst is in some sense (notionally) ideally benevolent and does represent a kind of reality check, although the
analyst is not, of course, the omnipotent Creator of all that
is, and thus in a position of unique and unquestioned authority, and obviously is not omniscient. A further and absolutely
crucial difference is that an essential part of the process of
analysis is that moral demands are imaginatively suspended.
See also Lear, *Love and Its Place in the Universe*.

6. In thinking about the issues raised in this paragraph I
have benefited greatly from Cottingham's *Philosophy and the
Good Life*.

7. Augustine *Confessiones* 10. 16.

8. See Kierkegaard, *Concluding Unscientific Postscript.*

9. This is perhaps an instructive instance of the general difficulties involved in trying to interpret segments of the history of philosophy in a historical way, and of the dilemma such an enterprise encounters.

10. In the modern Western world psychoanalysis is probably the closest analogue to traditional forms of spirituality, a mechanism for pursuit of a radically private good that is held to be of unique and perhaps overwhelming importance.

11. Augustine *De civ. Dei.* 20.2.

12. Augustine *De civ. Dei* 1.18.

13. See Hegel, *Enzyklopädie der philosophischen Wissenschaften* (Frankfurt: Suhrkamp, 1970) §§ 381–86.

14. I make no historical or causal claims about the sequence of stages I describe; they constitute no more than a logical or analytic typology. It is essential for Christianity that the fundamental metaphysical principle of the universe is a transcendent personal god, or rather a personal god who is *both* transcendent *and* immanent. This means that with a little pushing and shoving one can accommodate even pantheistic forms of spirituality in the scheme as something that can reasonably be classified relative to Christianity, since these forms of spirituality generally recognize an immanent deity. Buddhist spirituality, which lacks any god whatsoever, does fall outside the scheme. I am grateful to Fred Neuhouser for pointing out deficiencies in my original discussion here.

15. Although the emperor Julian (*Oratio 6*) seems to have tried to interpret Diogenes as an early representative of the kind of pagan spirituality he was attempting to establish as a form of competition to Christianity.

16. See, esp., *Jenseits von Gut und Böse* § 26.

17. Nietzsche *Zur Genealogie der Moral, Dritte Abhandlung* § 12.

18. Augustine *De civ. Dei* 13. 13; 14.23, 26.

19. There is a slightly different strand of connection between revulsion and spiritual power that emerges in the re-
curring stories about the revolting origins of such power.
Thus, in the medieval legend, Gregory is especially qualified
to become Pope because he is the child of brother-sister in-
cest and also has an incestuous relation with his mother/aunt
(cf. the modern version in Mann, *Der Erwählte*). Cf. Catullus
90 on the need for an especially powerful *magus* to be born
of an incestuous union. Cf. also Parry, "Sacrificial Death and
the Necrophagous Ascetic."

20. Kolnai, "Der Ekel," pp. 561–69.

21. Again, in *this* context it is irrelevant whether anyone
ever was able to do any of these things; what is interesting is
that things like this were widely taken to represent a perfectionist ideal. Weber is, in general, extremely enlightening on
this topic. See his *Wirtschaft und Gesellschaft*, and Zweiter
Teil, Kapitel 5. §§ 10–11, as well as the "Einleitung" and
the famous "Zwischenbetrachtung" of "Die Wirtschaftsethik
der Weltreligionen," in *Gesammelte Aufsätze zur Religionssoziologie*.

22. See also Moore, *Privacy*, p. 12.

23. *Confessiones* 6.3.

24. I should perhaps note that I have bracketed out of my
discussion another aspect of this, that is, Augustine's experience of God with his mother at Ostia, which seems to include
some momentary silencing of the static that makes communication between human persons mostly a matter of conjec-
ture (*Confessiones* 9.10). I leave this out of the discussion not

because I think it unimportant, but because I do not know what to make of it philosophically.

25. It is, of course, an extremely important issue as to who is considered to belong to the group of those who form what I have called the relevant "universe of discourse."

CHAPTER V. LIBERALISM

1. Brown, *Augustine of Hippo*, p. 240; cf. Rist, *Augustine*, pp. 239–45.

2. Rüdiger Bittner raised this objection in correspondence.

3. See Constant's discussion of the political significance of the historical expansion of commercial activities, consumer goods, and private activities in his "La liberté des anciens comparée à celle des modernes," in *De la liberté chez les modernes*, pp. 493–515.

4. Cf. Wolff, *The Poverty of Liberalism*.

5. "[*Verbrechen*] *wodurch einer gantzen Republick, oder Stadt und andern Gemeine* geschadet. . . . sind z.E. alle Arten Ketzereyen, Aufruhr, Mord, Todschlag, Ehebruch, Hurerey, Diebstahl u.a" ("[*Crimes*] *by which a whole commonwealth, city, or other community is harmed such as any form of heresy, rioting, murder, homicide, adultery, fornication, larceny, etc.*" [trans. RG]) from a *Universal-Lexicon* of 1740, edited by Johann Heinrich Zedler (as cited in Hölscher, *Öffentlichkeit und Geheimnis*, p. 76).

6. Bell, *The Cultural Contradictions of Capitalism*.

7. I consider here only one aspect of liberalism: its doctrine of public and private. From the fact that this fragment has a self-reinforcing character, it does not, of course, follow

that "liberalism" construed as a broader doctrine is equally self-reinforcing or even consistent.

8. Two recent excellent books on Dewey's political philos-ophy are Westbrook, *John Dewey and American Democracy*; and Ryan, *John Dewey and the High Tide of American Liberal-ism*, 1995.

9. Dewey, *The Public and Its Problems*, pp. 12 ff. 15 f.

10. Older histories of this include Habermas, *Struktur-wandel der Öffentlichkeit*; and Koselleck, *Kritik und Krise*. More recent work includes that by Negt and Kluge, *Öffentlichkeit und Erfahrung*. All these works devote particu-lar attention to the institutional context and sociological structuring of the "public realm."

11. Kant has great hopes for the salutary effect of public-ity in international affairs. See his "Zum Ewigen Frieden."

12. De Tocqueville, in his *La démocratie en Amérique* (2.14), speaks of the potential "tyrannie de la majorité" and Mill follows him in this (*On Liberty*, chap. 1).

13. Hegel's argument for the family as a necessary struc-ture of rational human life depends on the claim that only in a structure like the family, which has limitations of access built into it, can a human individual develop the appropriate feelings of self-affirmation and self-worth. Cf. his *Grund-linien zur Philosophie des Rechts* §§ 142–81.

14. Marx, *Deutsche Ideologie*, part 3.

15. Von Humboldt, *Ideen zu einem Versuch, die Gränzen der Wirksamkeit des Staats zu bestimmen*, p. 17. Since von Hum-boldt later in life became the minister of culture in Prussia responsible for a major reform of the educational system and the founding of the university in Berlin that today bears his name, it is clear that he eventually changed his views. Note that de Tocqueville has a sociological version of "antipater-

nalism" that focuses on the issue of municipal autonomy and on opposition to what he calls "la tutelle administrative" (*L'ancien régime et la Révolution*, book 2, esp. chap. 3).

16. Schlegel, *Lucinde*, pp. 32f. So not all romantics shared the more strenuous forms of the doctrine of "self-development." For a more recent and more politically focused version of a similar view, see Kazimir Malevitch, *La paresse comme vérité effective de l'homme*, trans. R. Gayrand (Paris: Editions Allia, 1999 [originally, 1921]).

17. This form of antipaternalism is most commonly associated with Isaiah Berlin (cf. *Four Essays on Liberty*, esp. "Two Concepts of Liberty," section 6). I discuss this further in my "Freedom as an Ideal," *Proceedings of the Aristotelean Society* (supplementary volume).

18. Wolff's *In Defense of Anarchism* is devoted to the question of the state's moral authority but illustrates this point *en passant* in an extreme form.

19. I am very grateful to Robert Pippin for discussions of this topic.

20. Usually the ideal of *fraternité* is interpreted to mean that people share as brothers, and to designate some notion of mutual aid, mutual benevolence, and so on. A society can, of course, in principle, be composed of free and equal members who are indifferent to one another, so the third ideal is not superfluous. It is also the case that fraternity does not obviously imply equality since relations between brothers in many societies are not egalitarian but hierarchical, with the oldest lording it over the younger; cf. Stewart, *In the Time of the Gypsies*, p. 55, on the contrast between relations between brothers among Magyar peasants and Gypsies in rural Hungary. Brothers do not always share with each other and are not always mutually benevolent (e.g., Polyneikes and

Eteokles). What does seem to be more widespread is that the barriers of shame and disgust may be lower between brothers than between nonsiblings.

21. In addition, one may wonder whether the appearance of free, self-validating rational consensus might not mask darker realities even in advanced and affluent societies.

22. To be a full-blown "subject" in Lukács' sense is to satisfy a stronger condition than simply being a "public" in Dewey's sense, because a "public" need not be conscious of itself as such—not everyone who will be affected by new cycling regulations may know that they will be—but a full-blown "subject" is self-conscious. Still, I think the application to Dewey will be clear.

23. Hobbes, *Leviathan*, chap. 14.

24. For instance, Nietzsche *Jenseits von Gut und Böse*. §§ 1–23; or *Götzen-Dämmerung* § "Die 'Vernunft' in der Philosophie" 74–79.

Chapter VI. Conclusion

1. Warren and Brandeis, "The Right to Privacy" in Schoeman, *Philosophical Dimensions of Privacy*, pp. 75–104). The historical background is given in Prosser's "Privacy," also in Schoeman, *Philosophical Dimensions of Privacy*, pp. 104–56.

2. Thompson, *"The Right to Privacy,"* in Shoeman, *Philosophical Dimensions of Privacy*, pp. 272–90.

3. For a Roman historian's conception of the view from Roman-occupied Britain, see Tacitus *Agricola* 30–32.

4. In fairness to Plato one should note that he was well aware of the highly problematic nature of his claim, and the need to deploy the weightiest and most sustained forms of

philosophical argumentation—virtually the whole of the *Republic*—to make it convincing.

5. Rorty, *Contingency, Irony, and Solidarity* (esp. "Private Irony and Liberal Hope"). I would suggest that it is precisely this retention of the public/private distinction that vindicates Rorty's claim to be a true heir (i.e., one of the many possible legitimate heirs) to the tradition of liberalism.

6. It is odd that Rorty, who has such salutary things to say about the inconsequence of the distinction between "subjective" and "objective" (see his *Philosophy and the Mirror of Nature*, esp. part 3), should fall prey to what seems to be an even more insubstantial version of the same thing.

7. Imagine what it would have been like to live in Asia Minor in the second century, knowing that a significant number of your neighbors were reading the book of the New Testament called *Apocalypse/Revelation*.

8. Hegel, *Phänomenologie des Geistes*, pp. 137–77; cf. Siep, "Der Kampf um Anerkennung: Zu Hegels Auseinandersetzung mit Hobbes in den Jenaer Schriften."

9. Nietzsche, *Die Fröhliche Wissenschaft* § 283.

10. Recently the most notable theorist in the present generation of the "Frankfurt School," A. Honneth, has developed this line in a highly systematic way in his *Der Kampf um Anerkennung*. Isaiah Berlin at least recognized the issue in "Two Concepts of Liberty," section 6, in his *Four Essays on Liberty*.

11. Nietzsche, *Jenseits von Gut und Böse.* § 44 and passim.

12. Hobbes, *Leviathan*, chap. 6.

13. Note that I am not at all interested in the specifically ontological issues about realism, but in "realism" as a kind of methodological strategy, a view about how, in what order, one should proceed or think of oneself as proceeding.

14. There are, of course, matters for art historical theories, heraldic theories, theories of folklore, and so on, to track.

15. This is a point that has been made repeatedly and with depressing persuasiveness by John Dunn in various writings, perhaps most fully in *Western Political Thought in the Face of the Future*.

REFERENCES

Editions of Older Works

Oxford Classical Texts (OCT) for Aristophanes (Hall/Geld-art), Aristotle (*Politica*: Ross), Catullus (Mynors), Diogenes Laertius (Long, 1964), Euripides (Murray), Herodotos (Hude), Martial (Lindsay), Plato (Duke, Hicken, Nicoll, Robinson, and Strachan [1995] for *Apology* and *Crito*; Burnett for the rest), Tacitus (Winterbottom and Ogilvie, 1975), and Thucydides (Jones-Powell); Teubner for Augustine (Skutella [1934] for *Confessiones*; Dombart/Kalb [1928/29] for *de Civitate Dei*), Julian (Hertlein, 1875), and Appian (Mendelssohn/Viereck, 1905).

Modern Works

Ball, T., J. Farr, and R. Hanson, eds. 1989. *Political Innovation and Conceptual Change*. Cambridge: Cambridge University Press.

Bell, D. 1976. *The Cultural Contradictions of Capitalism*. London: Heinemann.

Berlin, I. 1969. *Four Essays on Liberty*. Oxford: Oxford University Press.

Bok, S. 1983. *Secrets: On the Ethics of Concealment and Revelation*. New York: Pantheon.

Brown, P. 1967. *Augustine of Hippo*. Berkeley: University of California Press.

Brown, P. 1988. *The Body and Society.* New York: Columbia University Press.

Brunner, O., W. Conze, and R. Koselleck, 1972 ff. *Geschichtliche Grundbegriffe: Historisches Lexikon zur politisch-sozialen Sprache in Deutschland.* 9 vols. Stuttgart: Klett.

Constant, B. 1980 [1814]. *De l'esprit de la conquête et de l'usurpation* in *De la liberté chez les modernes: Écrits politiques.* Edited by Gauchet. Paris: Hachette.

————. 1980 [1814]. "De la liberté des anciens comparée à celle des modernes." In *De la liberté chez les modernes: Écrits politiques.* Edited by Gauchet. Paris: Hachette.

Cottingham, J. 1998. *Philosophy and the Good Life.* Cambridge: Cambridge University Press.

Dewey, J. 1927. *The Public and Its Problems.* New York: Holt.

Dodds, E. R. 1951. *The Greeks and the Irrational.* Berkeley: University of California Press.

Douglas, M. 1966. *Purity and Danger.* London: Routledge.

Drexler, H. 1988. *Politische Grundbegriffe der Römer.* Darmstadt: Wissenschaftliche Buchgesellschaft.

Dudley, D. 1998. *A History of Cynicism.* 2nd ed. London: Duckworth.

Duerr, H.-P. 1988. *Nacktheit und Scham.* Frankfurt/M: Suhrkamp.

————. 1990. *Intimität.* Frankfurt/M: Suhrkamp.

————. 1993. *Obszönität und Gewalt.* Frankfurt/M: Suhrkamp.

Dunn, J. 1993. *Western Political Theory in the Face of the Future.* 2nd ed. Cambridge: Cambridge University Press.

Elias, N. 1981 [1936]. *Über den Prozeß der Zivilisation.* 2 vols. Frankfurt/M: Suhrkamp.

Freud, S. 1974 [1905]. *Drei Abhandlungen zur Sexualtheorie* in *Sigmund Freud Studienausgabe*. Vol. 5. Frankfurt/M: Fischer.

————. 1974 [1929]. *Das Unbehagen in der Kultur* in *Sigmund Freud Studienausgabe*. Vol. 9. Frankfurt/M: Fischer.

Gauchet, M., ed. 1980 [1814]. *De la liberté chez les modernes: Écrits politiques*. Paris: Hachette.

Geuss, R. 1995. "Freedom as an Ideal." *Proceedings of the Aristotelean Society* (Supplementary Volume).

————. 1999. *Parrots, Poets, Philosophers, and Good Advice*. London: Hearing Eye.

Glare, P.G.W. 1968–1982. *Oxford Latin Dictionary*. Oxford: Oxford University Press.

Goulet-Cazé, M.-O. 1986. *Ascèse Cynique*. Paris:Vrin.

Goffman, E. 1963. *Behaviour in Public Places*. New York: Free Press.

————. 1963. *Stigmas: Notes on the Management of Spoiled Identity*. London: Penguin.

————. 1959. *Presentation of Self in Everyday Life*. London: Pelican.

————. 1974. *Frame Analysis: An Essay on the Organization of Experience*. London: Penguin.

Green, D. 1998. *Language and History in the Early Germanic World*. Cambridge: Cambridge University Press.

Halbertal, M., and A. Margalit. 1992. *Idolatry*. Cambridge, Mass.: Harvard University Press.

Habermas, J. 1962. *Strukturwandel der Öffentlichkeit*. Neuwied/Berlin: Luchterhand.

Hegel, G.W.F. 1970 [1830]. *Enzyklopädie der philosophischen Wissenschaften*. In *Werke in zwanzig Bänden*. Edited by Moldenhauer and Michel. Frankfurt/M: Suhrkamp.

Hegel, G.W.F. 1970 [1821]. *Grundlinien zur Philosophie des Rechts* in *Werke. In zwanzig Bänden.* Edited by E. Moldenhauer and Michel. Frankfurt/M: Suhrkamp.

———. 1970 [1807]. *Phänomenologie des Geistes.* In *Werke in zwanzig Bänden.* Edited by E. Moldenhauer and K. Michel. Frankfurt/M: Suhrkamp.

Hobbes, T. 1996 [1651]. *Leviathan.* 2nd ed. Edited by Richard Tuck. Cambridge: Cambridge University Press.

Hölscher, L. 1979. *Öffentlichkeit und Geheimnis.* Stuttgart: Klett Cotta.

Honneth, A. 1992, *Der Kampf um Anerkennung.* Frankfurt/M: Suhrkamp.

Kant, I. 1968 [1795]. "Zum Ewigen Frieden." In *Immanuel Kant Werkausgabe.* Vol. 11. Frankfurt/M: Suhrkamp.

———. 1977 [1790]. *Kritik der Urteilskraft.* In *Immanuel Kant Werkausgabe.* Vol. 10. Frankfurt/M: Suhrkamp.

Kantorowicz, E. H. 1957. *The King's Two Bodies.* Princeton, N.J.: Princeton University Press.

Kierkegaard, S. 1992 [1846]. *Concluding Unscientific Postscript.* Translated by H. Hong and E. Hong. Princeton, N.J.: Princeton University Press.

Kolnai, A. 1929. "Der Ekel." In *Jahrbuch für Philosophie und phänomenologische Forschung.* Tübingen: Niemeyer.

Koselleck, R. 1976. *Kritik und Krise.* 2nd ed. Frankfurt/M: Suhrkamp.

Kristeva, J. 1980. *Pouvoirs de l'horreur.* Paris: Seuil.

Lear, J. 1990. *Love and Its Place in the Universe.* New York: Farrar, Straus, and Giroux.

Lukács, G. 1968 [1923]. *Geschichte und Klassenbewußtsein.* Neuwied /Berlin: Luchterhand.

Malevitch, K. 1999 [1921]. *La paresse comme vérité effective de l'homme*. Paris: Éditions Allia.

Mann, T. 1967 [1951]. *Der Erwählte*. Frankfurt/M: Fischer.

Marx, K. 1953. *Grundrisse der Kritik der politischen Ökonomie*. Berlin: Dietz Verlag.

———. 1957 ff. *Werke*. Berlin: Dietz Verlag.

Meier, C. 1970. *Die Entstehung des Begriffs "Demokratie."* Frankfurt/M: Suhrkamp.

———. 1986. *Caesar*. Munich: Deutscher Taschenbuch Verlag.

Meinecke, F. 1924. *Die Idee der Staatsräson*. Munich: Oldenbourg.

Menninghaus, W. 1999. *Ekel*. Frankfurt/M: Suhrkamp.

Mill, J. S. 1989 [1859]. *On Liberty*. In *On Liberty and Other Writings*. Edited by S. Collini. Cambridge: Cambridge University Press.

Miller, W. 1997. *The Anatomy of Disgust*. Cambridge, Mass.:Harvard University Press.

Moore, B. 1984. *Privacy*. Armonk, N.Y.: M.E. Sharpe.

Negt, O., and Kluge, A. 1972. *Öffentlichkeit und Erfahrung*. Frankfurt/M: Zweitausendeins.

Nicolet, C. 1976. *Le métier de citoyen dans la Rome republicaine*. 2d ed. Paris: Gallimard.

Niehues-Pröbsting, H. 1979. *Der Kynismus des Diogenes und der Begriff des Kynismus*. Munich: Fink.

Nietzsche, Fr. 1967 ff. [1872]. *Die Geburt der Tragödie aus dem Geiste der Musik*. In *Kritische Gesamt-Ausgabe*. Vol. 1. Edited by Colli and Montinari. Berlin: de Gruyter.

———. 1967 ff. [1882]. *Die Fröhliche Wissenschaft*. In *Kritische Gesamt-Ausgabe*. Vol. 3. Edited by G. Colli and M. Montinari. Berlin: de Gruyter.

Nietzsche, Fr. 1967 ff. [1886]. *Jenseits von Gut und Böse.* In *Kritische Gesamt-Ausgabe.* Vol. 5. Edited by G. Colli and M. Montinari. Berlin: de Gruyter.

————. 1967 ff. [1887]. *Zur Genealogie der Moral.* In *Kritische Gesamt-Ausgabe.* Vol. 5. Edited by Colli and Montinari. Berlin: de Gruyter.

————. 1867 ff. [1888]. *Götzen-Dämmerung.* In *Kritische Ges-amt-Ausgabe.* Vol. 6. Edited by Colli and Montinari. Berlin: de Gruyter.

Parry, J. 1982. "Sacrificial Death and the Necrophagous Ascetic." In *Death and the Regeneration of Life.* Edited by Bloch and J. Parry. Cambridge: Cambridge University Press.

Prosser, W. 1984 [1960] "Privacy." In F. Schoeman, *Philosophical Dimensions of Privacy.* Cambridge: Cambridge University Press.

Rist, J. 1994. *Augustine.* Cambridge: Cambridge University Press.

Rorty, R. 1979. *Philosophy and the Mirror of Nature.* Princeton, N.J.: Princeton University Press.

————. 1989. *Contingency, Irony, and Solidarity.* Cambridge: Cambridge University Press.

Rosenkranz, K. 1979 [1853]. *Die Ästhetik des Häßlichen.* Reprint. Darmstadt: Wissenschaftliche Buchgesellschaft.

Ryan, A. 1995. *John Dewey and the High Tide of American Liberalism.* London: Norton.

Schlegel, Fr. 1985 [1799]. *Lucinde.* Munich: Goldmann.

Schoeman, F. 1984. *Philosophical Dimensions of Privacy.* Cambridge: Cambridge University Press.

Siep, L. 1974. "Der Kampf um Anerkennung: Zu Hegels Auseinandersetzung mit Hobbes in den Jenaer Schriften." In *Hegel-Studien 9.*

Skinner, Q. 1989. "The State." In *Political Innovation and Conceptual Change*. Edited by T. Ball, J. Farr, and R. Hanson. Cambridge: Cambridge University Press.

Sontheimer, W., and K. Ziegler. 1975. *Der kleine Pauly*. 5 vols. Munich: Deutscher Taschenbuch Verlag.

Stewart, M. 1997. *In the Time of the Gypsies*. Boulder, Colo.: Westview.

Suerbaum,W. 1979. *Vom antiken zum frühmittelalterlichen Staatsbegriff*. Münster: Aschendorffsche Verlagsbuchhandlung.

Thomson, Judith Jarvis. 1984 [1975]. "The Right to Privacy." In F. Schoeman, *Philosophical Dimensions of Privacy*. Cambridge: Cambridge University Press.

Tocqueville, A. de 1951 [1835/40]. *De la démocratie en Amérique* in *Oeuvres, papiers et correspondances*. Edited by J.-P. Meyer. Paris: Gallimard.

―――. 1967 [1856]. *L'ancien régime et la Révolution*. Paris: Gallimard.

Veyne, P. 1976. *Le pain et le cirque*. Paris: Seuil.

Von Humboldt, W. 1960 [1792]. *Ideen zu einem Versuch, die Gränzen der Wirksamkeit des Staats zu bestimmen* in *Werke in fünf Bänden*. Edited by Flitner and Giel. Stuttgart: Cotta.

Walzer, M. 1983. *Spheres of Justice*. New York: Basic Books.

S. Warren., and L. Brandeis. 1984 [1890]. "The Right to Privacy." In F. Schoeman, *Philosophical Dimensions of Privacy*.

Weber, M. 1934. *Gesammelte Aufsätze zur Religionssoziologie*. Tübingen: Mohr.

―――. 1956. *Wirtschaft und Gesellschaft*. Tübingen: Mohr.

―――. 1980. *Gesammelte politische Schriften*. Tübingen: Mohr.

Westbrook, R. 1991. *John Dewey and American Democracy.* Ithaca: Cornell University Press.

Wilamowitz-Moellendorff, U. 1909. *Euripides Herakles.* 2nd ed. Berlin: Weidmann'sche Buchhandlung.

Williams, B. 1993. *Shame and Necessity.* Berkeley: University of California Press.

Wirszubski, C. 1950. *Libertas as Political Ideal at Rome.* Cambridge: Cambridge University Press.

Wolff, R. P. 1968. *The Poverty of Liberalism.* Boston: Beacon.

Wolff, R. B. 1970. *In Defense of Anarchism.* New York: Harper and Row.

INDEX

145